About the Author

Mitchell Creed was convicted of a planned robbery – in company, circa 2009 having grown up in various parts of Australia due to a situation involving his parents and the Law he inherited a penchant for the nomadic lifestyle later in life, in fact his family often jokingly refer to him as 'the itinerant'. During his travels he never seemed to be grounded or find a calling until this one particularly dark period at rock bottom when he just decided to execute a heist.

Following a relatively short amount of preparation and planning, he pulled his first successful job, no one else was involved nor present and he was in and out in around twenty minutes carrying over eighty thousand dollars in cash and change.

Whilst incarcerated Mr Creed was diagnosed with Bi-Polar

disorder and upon the administration of the correct medication changed for the better virtually overnight, not hoping to blame his behaviour on his illness Mr Creed has penned this book in the hopes of inspiring misguided youths and would-be criminals to a higher purpose, one of honesty and freedom.

Despite his successes, he never reflects on his "career" with pride, in fact he is deeply ashamed at what he has done and ever since has remained adamant that his criminal career is over. He now resides in NSW where he is extremely fortunate to have rebuilt his life and thankful every day, for the opportunities that a successful reformation has afforded him, including acceptance into university.

Today he has a large and growing property portfolio, pays his taxes, donates to several charities and gives blood, he even has all his points on his driver's license.

Above all the author is thankful for the strong friendships and family bonds that have remained despite all his self-nullifying choices of the past!

Anonymity

Mitchell Creed

Anonymity

Olympia Publishers
London

www.olympiapublishers.com
OLYMPIA PAPERBACK EDITION

Copyright © Mitchell Creed 2024

The right of Mitchell Creed to be identified as author of this work has been asserted in accordance with sections 77 and 78 of the Copyright, Designs and Patents Act 1988.

All Rights Reserved

No reproduction, copy or transmission of this publication may be made without written permission. No paragraph of this publication may be reproduced, copied or transmitted save with the written permission of the publisher, or in accordance with the provisions of the Copyright Act 1956 (as amended).

Any person who commits any unauthorised act in relation to this publication may be liable to criminal prosecution and civil claims for damage.

A CIP catalogue record for this title is available from the British Library.

ISBN: 978-1-80439-879-1

This book is a memoir. It reflects the author's present recollections of experiences over time. Some names and characteristics have been changed, some events have been compressed, and some dialogue has been recreated.

First Published in 2024

**Olympia Publishers
Tallis House
2 Tallis Street
London
EC4Y 0AB**

Printed in Great Britain

Dedication

This book and it's Author's profits are dedicated to the victims of crime in Australia.

Acknowledgements

This book is a personal manifesto detailing the planning, execution, both successful and otherwise, of criminal enterprises and events and also includes a first-hand account from inside some Australian high security correctional centres, including solitary confinement and a delightful stint in the criminally insane unit. All names, states and venues have been changed for both the protection of those mentioned and to avoid self-incrimination. I will attempt to impart an understanding of my situation on those of you with clean consciences and for those of you who believe crime, particularly violent crime, is acceptable I hope to enlighten you on your folly, to an extent. I'd also like to mention that any and all profit generated by this book to the author Mr Creed (also a pseudonym) will be going to the National Crime Victim Law Institute.

Chapter 1
The Beginning of the End

I was lying in dewy grass in the middle of the oval in the dark looking through the 3Xs binos when I heard BA's voice crackle over the comms… "Girly man's on the move, so far I count him plus another three". His voice was calm and professional but inside his heart must've been racing. It was his first job and although it wasn't my first and my strike rate so far was one hundred percent this was different. Usually, I worked alone, no partner, no witnesses, no trail and 'my' ticker was about to give me a freakin conniption. The reasons for this were many, this was the first time third parties would be involved and there were already too many variables. This didn't sit well with me as prior to this job I considered my "work" as victimless crimes whereby the only casualties were the insurance agencies which I've always maintained are the real bad guys. To quote a saying "If something's done out of love it's beyond good and evil" and I really 'Love' working two to three hrs for a 120K pay day or in this case eight minutes and forty-two seconds, not counting prep time and dry runs. We'd cased the target on and off for the last couple of months and considered every conceivable situation. I'd even done hazard analysis and risk management on the job and factored in potential variables, this was it, tonight was go time, we wouldn't get a chance like this again for a long while. So whilst I laid there clad in black going over my mental checklist I imagined in my mind's eye how it would unfold. A few weeks earlier we'd setup with the intention of pulling the job that night though we were unsure of the number and ETA of cleaning staff. The target was one of many venues in town with hundreds of pokie machines, three bars a restaurant and a TAB. On the earlier attempt I'd gone in as a patron in disguise entering through the smoking area avoiding the "only" camera in this multi-million-dollar club and adjourning to the coffee room where I hid under a stage until closing . I remember being wedged under a the stage for hours talking to BA on the comms and having to piss into a salad dressing bottle I'd brought along specifically for that purpose. So after closing I let BA in and we waited to find that there were no less than four staff in unknown areas within the club so we aborted.

Obviously we needed to rethink and approach this differently, initially I'd planned on pulling the job using my usual formula, here in Oz crims call them 'sneaks' in the states they're known as jobs 'on the prowl' anyway given the nature of the vault and the window I'd need to deal with it I decided to recruit BA. As I mentioned earlier sneak jobs didn't affect my conscience too badly as they were merely victimless crimes. This job however was rapidly becoming something else. Believe it or not BA and my primary concern first and foremost was the safety and welfare of the staff, the last thing we wanted was for one of them to have a heart attack. Not only as we are human with feelings but also because in the event that things went tits up, we'd be in a shite load more trouble. I know it would never justify what we did but there are many reasons why I reluctantly decided to go ahead with the job in this way, not the least of which was the way a certain staff member had interfered in my life and cost me my job (or cover). The guy in question was not particularly good at his job and to top off his incompetence upon learning of my relationship with a mutual acquaintance he began harassing her to the point where I was about to beat the living snot out of him. Fortunately for him she talked me out of it, unfortunately for all parties once she saw my dark side she left me, hence the life changing decision, again this does not justify what we did.

This night BA and I decided on the fly to detain the three staff as they left the venue, direct them back inside and have them open the vault, restrain them and get the hell out of dodge. I worked my way around to the exit while BA monitored the staff and gave me continuous situation reports and as they left we converged on their position. BA – "right guys this is a robbery, lay on the ground and no one gets hurt!"

The two girls complied immediately meanwhile Girly man was off and screaming leaving the actual girls to fend for themselves, knowing him like I did it was no surprise. His little legs had sprinted him about 10 metres so after about five or six strides I was on him and had secured him by his tie and gently put his arm in a soft lock behind his back. In the calmest heavily fake German accent I could muster I said – "Relax fella vee are not going to hurt any one and the money is inshhuured, we'll be gone before you know it!"

At this stage we are about three minutes in, BA and I herded the staff back inside constantly reassuring them that they will be fine. BA and I were, I don't like to use the word threatening but, operating on the premise that they believed we were armed, in reality BA had a pistol shaped piece of wood that he never produced and I had nothing but flex cuffs. After asking Girly man if there were any other staff in the venue and getting only inaudible whimpering as a response I once again reassured him in my fake accent, I wouldn't have had to speak at all if he wasn't such a terrified wreck, then one of the girls spoke up and mentioned that there were another three cleaning staff which we decided girly man would call to while I waited by the door looking menacing.

When the staff came in I was out of their peripheral and I simply closed the door behind them and whilst they went into shock upon taking in the situation, again something I'm not proud of I simply explained that they would be fine and that we were just here for the money as I applied the large zip ties as flex cuffs, Anyway from here on in it's plain sailing, I left BA to watch the girls and took Girly man to contain the cleaning staff, one by one all three of them are secured in flex cuffs. At the five minute mark we open the vault, a seven by five foot steel reinforced door to a strong room which I know contains a safe that has somewhere between 90 and 150K. My hands are gloved but I insist that Girly man does the loading, I hand him the duffel bag that is capable of holding upto 50 ltrs or 30 kgs of cargo which was good because we needed every square inch of space. At the seven minute mark I return to BA Girly man in tow. We decided against locking the staff in the strong room for two reasons – A; it would be cruel and B; we don't want them to potentially suffocate. So we leg it leaving them in the main bar. BA and I spent the next 4 hrs counting and recounting the loot at the flop we found we had somewhere in the vicinity of 61K each. I have, or had, trouble sleeping at the best of times but as you can imagine I was pumped that night and fantasizing about shiny sports cars , cruises and European trips. Despite my instinct to head cross country there and then the plan was to depart in the morning, I would head interstate leaving the territory as I had a link to the target, and BA would continue as usual. In retrospect we should have both gone cross country, changed out the cash (I will detail this process later) and hopped a plane to anywhere but Oz. The next day I was interstate having taken some, though not enough, precautions – * Turning off my mobile removing the sim-card and battery * Changing out the sim from my laptops wireless * Only communicating with BA in vague terms via a social network or pay phone.

Now I'm usually fairly adamant that this life is nothing like Ocean's eleven or a Guy Ritchie flick but the following couple of weeks were a blur of high stakes poker, blackjack , shit loads of booze and a few other things I should probably omit. So following a couple of weeks of being a cashed up pleasure seeking adrenaline junkie fugitive I started to get a little lax on security and instead of ditching my car like I should have and buying a bomb or cheap bike I was driving around in a known car with the only evidence, 50 odd K of cash, in the boot. Next thing I know I'm enroot to see my cousin when my worst fears were realised, I saw flashing blue lights in the rear view knowing instantly what would follow I began to formulate a plan, not of escape but of misdirection and tactics that would make me look nuts and hopefully save BA's arse. So I'm sitting in my car in a trance like state of calm the acceptance and dreaded realisation of the deep deep trouble I'm in washing over me when a very nervous young constable approaches my window with his Glock pointed at the ground, it's not lost on me that his partner, who looks kind of like Mac from super troopers, is at the passenger side with his pistol drawn too. Officer – " Morning sir, this is an RBT!"

Me – "Really? Do you plan on shooting me if I'm drunk?"

Officer – "Please exit your vehicle sir?"

Me – "No worries"

Officer – "Anything in the car or on your person that we need to know about? Weapons or drugs?"

Me – "Drugs? um no officer I don't do drugs."

Officer – "We'll be conducting a search of the vehicle now."

Me – "Um I'm no lawyer officer, but don't you need a warrant or at least probable cause?"

Officer –"I have probable cause – I smell drugs!"

Me – "Yeah I think I smell something!"

Officer – "What?"

Me – "Never mind, listen I'll save you some trouble, my bags in the boot and no I don't have any weapons!"

While captain obvious searched the car Mac had his Glock pointed at my back while a special operations cop, who'd jumped out of a second unmarked car, was searching me just a little too enthusiastically. Must've looked odd an average looking guy flanked by heavily armed, black clad cops being searched in broad daylight, people must have thought I was a freakin serial killer or something! As it turns out I would soon discover despite my best attempt at a thick German accent Girly man had in fact ID'd me, and as the local cops back home still had no actual evidence they'd taken it upon themselves to plant bullets and shell casings in my apartment so as to give them the necessary authority to detain and extradite me back to the territory. In any case now they had 50K that I just happened to have in my boot so basically I was fucked. My plan was to act out a mental disorder so as to minimize my sentence and get leniency. I just hoped BA was clear of this cluster fuck! Turns out the detectives in this particular town were actually pretty cool despite the good cop bad cop routine though as I suspected one of them was an actual prick. So I'm in the interview room with D1 and D2, D1 is younger and reminds me a little of Cyril Figgis from the Archer cartoon series and D2 is the Prick. The three of us are sitting there quietly for what seems like 10 minutes before I finally ask "So can you guys tell me what this is about?"

Cyril – "Mitch, why don't you tell us about the money?"

Me –"Just saving it for a rainy day."

Prick –"Bullshit!"

Me –"Pardon?"

Prick – "I said that's bullshit, that cash is from a heist! A very violent one according to the locals!"

Oh great! Sounded like girly man and the local super troopers were going to push for the death sentence.

Me – "Are you saying I stole it?"

Prick – "They found ammo at your house genius!"

Me – "Really? Well I suspect once the CMC gets involved and re-examines this "evidence" not only will my prints be absent from said evidence but you "Geniuses" will have your prints all over it!"

This statement was one hundred percent true as I had never owned a gun or any ammo.

That night I started my psycho routine singing off key all night about the injustice of my predicament and not sleeping, basically driving everyone else nuts too. I wasn't overly worried about the cash as the truth was I'd already changed it out using casinos, banks and even a few foreign exchange branches which meant it was laundered and untraceable, some people may argue that it was already clean but it doesn't take a genius to know that the presence of staff DNA and prints would be a deal breaker, as far as these cops and the locals back home knew it really was mine and all they really had was some frightened little sycophants testimony that he'd picked my voice! No prints, no DNA, no footage, nada. My main concern was for BA who at the very least would be monitoring the news and by now would know of this shit storm. Cyril and Prick had told me that two D's from the territory would be jetting in in the morning, yay! After a long night of watch house Karaoke it was time to meet the boys from the bush. It was as if I was being introduced to an interstate version of Cyril and Prick! What? Did they grow these guys in labs or something? Same routine except the young guy looked like Shane Webke from seven news probably the same size too the guy was huge.

Webke – "Good morning Mitch, we hear you're having trouble sleeping?"

Me – "Morning Detective, yeah well it's a condition! Any way as I'm sure you can appreciate I'd really like to sort this whole mess out as quickly as possible."

The older guy looked like Niles from 'The Nanny'.

Niles – "You should get comfortable cause you're not going anywhere for a while!"

Later at the interview room after about a million coffees.

Webke – "Does the name Abraham Longley mean anything to you?"

Fuck! They had BA which meant we were fucked, there is no way he'd have changed out his cash or better, moved it somewhere safe.

Me – "Well we are good mates why? Is he all right?"

Niles – "Save it Mitch, we know it was you!"

Yes, yes they did, so my best course of action was to play up the nutjob routine and prepare myself for a lot of card playing, fighting, studying, reading and the occasional dirty, dirty cigarette.

Chapter 2
Inside

I spent the next couple of weeks being shipped back and forth between watch houses and prisons whilst waiting for extradition. The local cops didn't know how to handle my twenty-four-hour karaoke sessions and as I was driving everyone nuts I too was really losing it. Doctors will tell you it doesn't matter who you are if you're not sleeping it's not a question of if, but when will you become unhinged. While you are in the watch house which is more commonly used as a drunk tank you meet some colourful and interesting characters, for instance it's amazing how many heavily tattooed ethnic guys come in all hard and scary only to burst into tears the second the cage locks behind them, especially when their cell mate is a creepy looking sleep deprived karaoke enthusiast. It must have been about week three when the AFP showed up with Pol-Air (police airways) to fling me back up to the territory. Amazing even the feds used the D1 D2 formula! except this time they were both bad cops. D1 was a fit young fella who reminded me of a young Charlie Sheen, (possibly on steroids) D2 looked more like Ross Kemp and a Pom to boot. They slapped me in leg irons and made me shuffle towards a waiting six-seater, not too flash I was hoping for a Gulfstream, that was the last thing on my mind when I saw that it seemed as if the whole local department had turned up to see me off, must have been my singing voice. I was dying for a piss and of course the only option was to go right there and then in full view of the local piggery, some of the female staff could have done well as actors or models which didn't help, but made it strange to be on the receiving end of wolf whistles, not like I could file a sexual harassment complaint or anything. After my much-needed relief the pilot briefed us finishing with "Any questions gentleman?" to which I replied-

"Yes, how many parachutes on board and can I have one please?"

Ross Kemp- "Ha freakin ha, shut it Danny Ocean!"

Three hours later I was being received by the locals back in the Territory in their fortress of a watch house where I would be processed, printed, DNA tested, catalogued and assigned a number. I'd also be given the traditional initiation by six of the most pissed off cops I've ever met, usually a good flogging doesn't phase me too much but given my present state ie; no real sleep for a few weeks and the fact that I was having an actual real breakdown I honestly thought they were going to kill me. It got so bad that one of the feds told them that they didn't actually have anything solid on me yet and that I may in fact be innocent. One by one they came in an apologised.

Me- "Ha water under the bridge I said spitting a gob of blood on the floor!"

Meanwhile all the other detainees both male and female were screaming brutality and telling the cops they were fucked cause everyone was behind me. I honestly didn't care at this point and given the gravity of my breakdown I was starting to welcome death I didn't sing any karaoke that night, instead I wrote a confused and long winded letter to my dad which at the time made a lot of sense, in it I basically apologised profusely for all my shortcomings and hoped he could forgive me, knowing my old man he probably blamed himself for all my self-defeating behaviour. That letter writing session was the first time I had cried in years, and wouldn't again for at least two years which ironically was the duration of my stay in the big house. To this day I still don't know if dad ever got that letter or just how frigged up it was. The big house was pretty much what I'd expected, the average block had around 30-60 cells or churchies as we call them, a communal TV, basketball court in the yard and two officers or 'screws' to monitor us.

Each cell had a TV and a preset radio they were about 2 by 3 metres and the door consisted of a steel reinforced plate with a lock that is only accessible from the outside, one window which is airtight plexi glass or lexon. At least this was what the layout of the new sections of the prison were like, later I would find that the older areas were far worse but in a way better as if I was looking at serious time it would be much easier to bust out of, though still incredibly bloody hard! Anyone who's done time will be intimately familiar with the card games 'chop' and '41', I'm more partial to Texas hold'em myself so I soon convinced my new neighbours to learn how to play, the rest of the time I learned chop and read, did a little training and avoided trouble which wasn't easy at first as given my ploy to portray a wacko I'd been placed in the infamous 'special needs unit' aka the psycho unit, which was full of very sick people, Sex offenders, murderers, serial killers and at least one confirmed cannibal. One aspect of prison that still amazes me is the level of conniving bitchiness and back stabbing that goes on among allegedly hardened criminals. Particularly when said crims are in for stabbing some poor bastard over a hundred bucks and then they hear you are in for a 120K heist! In any case as it turned out the biggest hazard at this point was smoke inhalation as I would soon be transferred to 'the facility' a much scarier more secure actual insane asylum for criminals.

Chapter 3
The Facility

They say that moving house is one of the most stressful events you will endure! Trust me when you are being moved to 'the facility', it 'is!

On the ride over I made small talk with the screws and said "I hope you guys don't think I'm a rapist or something? I'm just a stupid robber!"

To which the screw replied – "To us each jobs the same and every crim is the same!, Doesn't matter to us if you're a paedophile or a thief".

It was at this point I realised that it was futile to attempt to explain to him what a huge insult that statement was. Because it came from a screw who basically had to be considerably dumber than average to get the job in the first place, and in all likely hood didn't even realise what he'd just implied. That was soon to be the least of my worries, upon arrival I was re-processed through several check points and grilled by the doctors and staff who are technically screws and nursing staff too, most of which are ex-military imports from the UK or the states. None of that concerned me, what concerned me was the insidious nature of my pre-detention briefing. Statements like "Avoid eye contact with the big one!" and "That guys been in that same room for six years" had me a little pre occupied. The person who 'hadn't left the room in six years' was a violent cannibal who didn't speak and was presently staring me out through an inch of plexi glass, as I was led out he gave me a disturbing grin revealing a set of modified canines that he'd apparently filed sharp back in his finger lickin days. Next up I met Scott, or at least observed him running around the lap track with his hands in customized shackles that looked like big soft mittens chained to his waist apparently he had a disorder that isn't as uncommon as you may expect where the patient believes absolutely that they are in fact a vampire and need to consume human blood. Later I would witness four big burley orderlies struggle to get all of Scott's 60 odd kilos to the ground to acuphase (that neato sedative that comes in a syringe that's configured like a little pistol) him and put him back in his cage. That night I met the rest of the gang who on first glance seemed to be quasi-normal though as you'd expect every one there, including yours truly, had some deep seeded issues. Over the coming weeks I would learn that my insomnia was a symptom of an underlying case of bipolar disorder. My doctor was pretty good and knew that I had been suffering for a long time, our sessions became a little comical as we both knew I wasn't totally innocent and until my solicitors told me that BA would be pleading guilty this is how it would continue. The Doc had a great sense of humour for a guy that had obviously seen and heard some bloody horrible stuff over the years and wasn't as clinically detached as I expected given that he regularly dealt with some just plain evil people. I'd quickly noticed that his left eye had suffered a trauma at some point that appeared to be in the shape of a human fingernail, no prizes for guessing what had happened. In the coming weeks I would learn that the seemingly semi normal group in the main section, where I was kept, ranged from simple car thieves with disorders to child killers to one particular guy who I initially felt sorry for that turned out to be rather proud of the fact that he had killed four homeless people using a freakin house brick.

During my ample time to reflect and analyse I found myself wondering how so many individuals could get themselves into this sort of predicament and why there wasn't more treatment available and the answer was obvious almost immediately, most folks don't know they have a disorder and/or don't know how to go about treating it and with those that do the system is struggling to cope with the sheer volume.

As previously mentioned the crazy unit back at the big house had quite a few candidates for 'the facility' however there simply isn't enough room to manage more than a dozen inmates at any given time.

Despite being in what most people, normal people, would deem a rather frightening environment I actually found some solace in the fact that I was out of general population and knew how the facility worked in that if there was a threat, which seemed unlikely given the drugs etcetera, I knew how to manage one.

It was amusing to note that the most irritable human

there was a guy that most would have observed on the street and thought nothing of, average height, weight, looks and the personality of a mute politician, however when I was in the middle of watching something on the facilities only television and the guy turned it off what happened next was very unexpected.

Having politely informed the inmate that I was watching that and turning it back on he immediately burst into a tirade of screaming through clenched teeth to the point where he was spitting and hurling his arms around the air like an epileptic Peter Garret.

The joke was on him though as I knew what would follow next-out came the orderlies with the acuphase and bang, what was a crazy screaming lunatic was now an unconscious twit being dragged off to his room for nap time.

I'd soon learn that the above mentioned psycho was the fore mentioned 'child killer' unfortunately for one young girl in her teens this nutjob had developed an obsession with her and in his mind if he couldn't have her no one could and as is not unusual he had some weird shrine in his cell covered with a collage of her pictures.

One of the things that creeped me out the most about the facility aside from the sterile environment, the drugs and 'oh yes' the psychos was the realisation that I in fact actually had a real problem.

However this was a blessing in disguise as it meant I

could be treated.

At this point I had no idea how long I'd been in the place and I'd given up hassling them about dates and current events. Though it wasn't long before I was shipped back to the big house, yay!

Chapter 4
Home Again

In Australia you can be held on remand (without trial) for up to three years! I've never claimed to be the most astute and philanthropic human rights activist or whatever but it seems a little odd that there is so much controversy surrounding asylum seekers and immigration (whom I actually really feel for by the way) when our own citizens can be subjected to this kind of hell basically without any real proof, and for those of you naive enough to think *'well they're all dirty crimes anyway'* let me assure you that that's not always the case! I mean if you follow the news closely enough you'd know this anyway. What pisses me off the most about this sort of thing though is the way the alleged perpetrator is treated prior to vindication only to have some page eleven small print retraction/article outlining the incompetence of the prosecution and bacon. When I got back to the slightly less 'funny' funny farm news quickly spread that I'd been to the scary place. My skin was as white as a sheet as I'd been wandering around that ward like a zombie for nearly nine months it turns out. Guys were coming up to me and asking "Hey Mitch what the fuck did they do to you in there bro? You don't look good man!" The rest of the offenders were giving me a wide birth like "I" was a psycho, but as I improved the screws had agreed to transfer me to the working unit *Yipee*! Believe it or not you do actually get paid in this unit, but before you get all angry at the system I should point out that it's basically slave labour and the "pay" is just around $20 AUD a week and all of it ends up going back into the system with our personal expenses ie; shaving and hygiene equipment extra food etc. However this setup is a great way to keep guys out of trouble and to make your time a little more bearable, usually, unless one of your co-workers is a fat wackjob with the mind of a child who is doing his best to look like, act like and actually constantly quote Chopper Reid. These sort of guys I actually find entertaining, this one in particular lets call him 'James' was so in love with Chopper he actually thought he was Chopper and wore his insecurities on his sleeve in the form of chopper tats, that were actual sleeves. This 140kg wad of man fat, totally oblivious to the fact that his cardio limits alone would mean most inside could kill him without breaking a sweat, had heard about my job, just so we are clear I made a point of only mentioning the nature of the job when asked and left out the amounts etc but the job had attracted a lot of attention and was fairly common knowledge by now, any way as James was more than a little slow I suspected that he had suffered some kind of head injury, and he was being overly friendly to me all the time which I knew was eventually going to mean trouble. I felt some semblance of liberation with this new classification that allowed me to "work", it meant that I would almost have a sense of daily purpose and structure and that I could accumulate some actual money if I so chose to, one of the guys I met transferred all of his earnings onto his phone account so that upon leaving he would be written a check, which I thought was a rather clever way of using the prison system as a small bank account, though at the end of the day I didn't really accumulate any surplus funds I just spent the extra $18.50 a week on biscuits and snacks but what it did show me was how little you need to keep yourself going which I later applied on the outside to live very frugally and save much more efficiently.

Work was the prison kitchen and I was the new dish pig soon to move up to the highly challenging section of food prep. One day I was working as a prep hand and had to go to the freezer to get something when I got there James and one of his underlings were waiting and, just as a joke they thought they'd start jabbing me with cucumbers like a couple of food fetish homos. I was on edge already and waiting for something like this and probably could have just laughed and left only James was blocking the door and that's when I got really pissed I grabbed both of them by the throat and jammed their fat heads against the freezer wall and in my best psycho villain voice said – "This is the part where you two fucktards either wake up to yourselves or get fisted, pull this shit again and you're fucking dead!" and pushed them out of the way before pissing of rather quickly as I was anticipating some backlash, turned out Mr wanna-be Chopper was even more of a pussy than I had given him credit as I didn't have any issues with him ever again.

The same couldn't be said for another hard arse in the unit who I eventually got into a real bust up with, I'm not one of these guys who never admits defeat so I'll be honest and tell you that this guy had me pretty fucked up but I'll

never know how it would have turned out because as I started to land a few, both of us pissing claret everywhere I got him by the collar and that's when the whole unit got into it pulling us apart and randoms throwing wild punches here, there and everywhere. I guess part of me knew that I was going to make it out of the system in one piece as I never fought anyone with my full abilities which sounds insane and any convict would tell you that you fight to win and kill if you have to, but despite all of the very serious consequences around my incarceration part of me never really felt like it was real or that I should worry, and I'd never want to kill anyone no matter what as that would mean I would not be
coming out for a very long time.

    I 'was' shitting myself a little though, not due to the fight or the fear of reprisals but simply because I knew there was a better than average chance I'd be visiting a real fucked up place that anyone with any sense will avoid like the plague, solitary confinement.

Chapter 5
Solitary Confinement

Just about everyone on planet earth old enough to know of this thing called solitary has imagined it, one would think, I had been dreading this prospect since I knew I'd be doing time. Let me tell you – nothing prepares you for it, I'd heard stories from both the inmates and the screws that when they built the jail they had an elite SAS unit placed inside posing as cons and their mission was to probe the security for flaws and even try to escape, according to the cons they were successful and according to the screws they weren't but during my stay in this fine establishment I dealt with many screws some of them more human than others and I found that the more honest and normal ones had a tendency to concede that these guys had in fact escaped which was a huge embarrassment to the screws as at the time most of them didn't even know they weren't actual prisoners and had treated them like snot. Any way I contemplated this story many times whilst laying in my new cell that consisted of cinderblock walls and a concrete floor with a foam mattress which is a single and took up most of the floor to give you an idea of the ample space provided, no sheets or covers and the lights are on 24/7 so they can observe you via the camera in the corner that actually follows your face around the room, on my wall located right below the camera in big black letters sure enough someone had written "Who dares wins!" which was really weird as whoever did this had access to a paint pen and also because they hadn't removed it. Even writing about this now I feel a strange queasiness at the thought of those days, weeks and even months spent in there. Following my bust up with old mate they'd basically frog marched us down to the DU, (detention unit) which is a PC way of saying solitary torture, put him in a cell at one end and me in a cell at the other. I'm not the biggest fan of people who make the career choice of prison guard or screw but I'll admit that I actually thought fairly highly of more than a few of them, but anyone that's been unfortunate enough to have served in solitary has had the displeasure of meeting the worst of the worst! These guys really are a sick bunch, they actually get off on causing misery and they needn't bother as the place is bad enough without more arseholes. They'll wake you up by running into your cell screaming like a drill sergeant at three in the morning sometimes do this four or five times the same night and if they really hate you as I discovered you will rapidly loose weight as all the food they give you will be open and tampered with, and 'I'm kind of glad they made it obvious as at least that way I knew not to put it in my mouth. Apparently these guys had trouble understanding the concept that says "we are here as punishment, not to be punished" I mean the fact that you have had everything taken away from you, no chance of sex, at least not the kind most of us are accustomed to, you're away from your loved ones and all this is supposed to rehabilitate you. What it actually does is eats away at your soul and if any normal person ends up doing serious time, trust me they won't be normal when they get out. This first stint in the hole turned out to only be a couple of weeks though it seemed like a year. I wish I could say that that was my time in the hole but unfortunately I'd be back and the next stint would make this one look like a day trip. Because of the expected reprisals following the fight instead of going back to the workers unit I got sent straight back to the looney bin, yay! Most of the original guys were still there but there were a few new faces, not very friendly faces I might add, just kept getting better and better, after about a month of watching some dickhead stand over everyone I'd finally had enough and in the middle of a training session he mouthed off next thing I know I've put a combo on him, just rabbit punches and a kick in the guts. The screws broke it up pretty fast but in hindsight it was a bloody stupid thing to do as straight away I knew I should have finished it there and then, this guy was by far the craziest fruit loop in the unit and he wasn't going away. I spent the next few days looking over my shoulder and always knowing where this guy was, then a few weeks had passed and I got a bit complacent. I'd taken my eyes of him for literally a couple of seconds when I was struck over the back of the head with a tray of hot Bolognese luckily I was still conscious as this prick had made a shiv which he then tried to put in my lung, I had turned just enough to put my right elbow in the path of the blade. next thing I know I've tackled this shit head to the floor, which is covered in my plasma mixed with Italian sauce, and as I'm punching the piss out of him he tried to fend me off with his right arm and I put him in a figure four arm bar, I tell you if the screws hadn't got me off then I would have totally fucked his shoulder forever, as it turns out I did pop it but the medics put it back in straight away pretty much. So one guess where I was heading after this little altercation. Despite the fact that I was obviously defending myself and I'd been stabbed I ended up doing about a month in the hole, yay! The medics had to constantly point at my wound that they'd packed with gauze and say to the screws "For fuck's sake look at his elbow, the poor bastards been stabbed!" Not only would the head screw not acknowledge this, but he suggested that I had started the whole thing and as luck would have it during our little fisty cuffs about three separate fights broke out, hence the month in solitary. What made this stint all that much worse was the fact that for the first couple of days all the guys from my unit involved in the blue were there with me and constantly wound each other up. This wouldn't have been a problem save for the sick bastard screws I mentioned earlier. They'd decided to focus their aggression on one particular inmate, a small indigenous guy who genuinely was very lost and probably not totally evil. I remember hearing them belting the absolute shit out of this poor bugger who was only about 5.5ft. gutless bastards, it was a real nightmare because at one point it sounded like they were doing more than just beating him. I didn't know what the hell to do and at this stage was still on the wrong meds which probably contributed to the decision to do something drastic in front of the camera to try and stop them. So I broke a broom handle in half (brooms were left in our cells in solitary as they often woke us up to sweep, for no apparent reason) and threw myself on it, I know crazy right? But it worked, they stopped and fortunately the broom had only penetrated slightly, these days there is only a slight hint of a scar. What really irked me about that whole situation was the fact that that poor little guy who'd obviously already had a tragic bloody life simply didn't understand what was happening and those freakin animal screws were too dumb to know it, the whole thing was perpetual, the more they beat him the more he protested and on and on it went. Any way most of the rest of my time in the hole is a blur as you can imagine, one thing I didn't mention was that during the day there is a second area of the cell they let you into, they call it yard time, sick bastards, basically it's just an area the same size as your cell but without a roof but lined with razor wire. During my month I'd perfected this ritual I had when it rained. What I'd do is lye on the concrete in my 'yard' in the rain and meditate and imagine the rain was cleansing all the hate and bad experiences off my body, it was totally Zen.

Chapter 6
Bloody Fisty Cuffs

One of the units I was transferred to was stocked with a diverse range of extremely young guys and the other end of the spectrum, guys that probably had senior's cards with a few odd ones like myself in between. When I first arrived it was obvious who thought he was the alpha, some generation Y with about half of his teeth that seemed to be the self-appointed DJ cranking the stereo every time a track that seemed to fit his profile came on, the profile of young delusional gangster whom on the outside would be clad in a tacky tracksuit, gold chain and TN Nike sneakers. To help paint a picture when ever this guy opened his mouth only Americanised gangster slang seemed to come out past his remaining peanut brittle looking teeth, must've had a bad Meth addiction before his time here though as mentioned it isn't impossible to get contraband inside either.

I could tell right away to be wary of this guy, not so much as he was a threat but he seemed to have a lot of followers in the form of guys so dumb they believed he was a leader which meant any altercation with him would mean trouble from all sides, I hadn't planned on having any issues with anyone in any event so I did my best to just play chess with a pretty cool indigenous Aussie guy that I met that called himself BT, every now and then BT and I would do some training to as we were about the same height and build he was a good spotter, there are no weights or equipment in the prisons I served in and we had to improvise with water filled 20ltr bottles and smaller containers etc, the rest of our sessions were just with our own body weight calisthenics type stuff.

When we usually trained as we were in a confined yard surrounded by extremely bored and unpredictable crims we would make a point of training facing one and other and watching each other's six, same thing whenever we played chess. It wasn't unusual to start training and no sooner than we start all of a sudden, every other monkey in there decides he wants to do some exercise including peanut mouth who would usually try his best to imitate Bruce Lee on the only heavy bag in the cell block yard, it was actually a bit sad as he did this one running fly kick over and over again which seemed to be the only tool in his tool kit, and while he hit hard with his Enter the Dragon impersonation that seemed to be the only reason that other inmates wanted to act like he was the Lion of the den. What really made it sad was he appeared to be sizing me up whenever he trained, after completing one of his little kicks he would land and immediately look at me as if to say 'I've get you covered'.

Peanut mouth while younger and presumably fitter, he wasn't, stood at about 177cm and I'd say 70kgs wringing wet in boots, without talking myself up, I can handle myself and I came in at the time around 99kgs and 185cm just on six foot-one so he was about as much risk to me, provided he wasn't armed, as my little sister.

So one day in the unit the inevitable happened, though not as I'd expected, it was actually my fault to an extent as I let this kids DJing get to me when he changed the station from a song that he deemed 'gay' that just so happened to be a track that my ex and I listened to, so I turned it back and immediately peanut mouth was up and ranting, flexing his little Bruce Lee arms calling me out. I wasn't about to get into it with gusto but I wasn't backing down either so predictably peanut mouth delivered his fly kick and as mental as it seems I just let it hit me right in the mouth, a collective 'Oooooooo!' let out through the unit as I just stood there then spat a little bit of blood on the concrete and asked- 'Is that it?' peanut mouth kept his fight stance and running his peanut mouth but he was backing away as he did so and his body language basically said 'Oh fuck!' any way he was saved by the bell as the guards came into the yard and started carrying on, we were obviously going to get marched up to the admin building to be interviewed and the guard nearest me told me to sit on the ground and when I said no he started yelling it as deeply and tough-guy like as he could I just yelled back in his face in a kiai 'I'm not a fucking dog!' and he immediately changed his tune, he was trying to assert his dominance over me and not only did he not have any but I didn't have any fucks to give about the repercussions of my disobedience as there was no need for me to sit on the ground in the first place.

So after being marched up to the admin building one by one a few "witnesses" came in too which really amazed me as before ever being inside a correctional centre it was my understanding that the last thing you ever wanted to appear to be was a snitch. These guys were all on team peanut mouth as they were from the shallow end of the gene pool so even before we went into separate interview rooms they were spouting comments like 'you're in for it now' and they were really referring to discipline from the guards not from themselves so you couldn't come across as a bigger bitch if you tried. When I entered my interview room it was the warden himself that interviewed me and for the first minute I just sat there and didn't say anything, eventually the warden asked 'so Mitch tell me what happened' to which I replied 'Nothing really, just some training that probably went a little overboard'. I could tell by the warden's expression that he respected my answer which wasn't really a surprise as all the bitches in the adjoining rooms would be carrying on with all manner of crazy takes on their version of events.

After that almost all of the guards I had contact with treated me like you would expect to be treated by a civil servant if you were in a post office or townhall, not with pleasantries or flattery but no disdain either, and the other prisoners in the unit gave me a wide birth, I'd actually been placed back in the same unit with peanut mouth and the others which seemed like it could be a big risk to me as I'm sure the little guy wanted to show he could hurt me somehow, even if it was through unfair means. BT had been transferred to another unit so I had no one to play chess with and found myself gravitating toward the older guys to perhaps seek some sort of wisdom around dealing with the servitude of time. Basically the general consensus was the same as my mantra already, do your time, stay out of trouble, keep busy.

I made sure I kept an eye on peanut mouth and his goons but it seemed they had no interest in me, any one that witnessed the altercation that had a brain would immediately recognise that his kick basically did nothing to me and that chances are I would obliterate him, in his mind however he had defeated me as I didn't really get into it with him because as previously mentioned I was doing my best to avoid trouble.

Unfortunately for one of the older baby boomers in the unit he must've assumed that he could spar with peanut mouth too and simply move on. This old guy actually had it all over peanut mouth and being an older guy afterward shook peanut mouth's hand and said 'all good champ' like there was some sort of honour between them. About two days later the old guy was in the yard against the wall in a siesta position when peanut mouth tipped boiling water from the unit urn all over his head and started stomping him and one of peanut mouth's underlings was doing the same to one of the old guy's friends just for sitting with him, it was horrible seeing a couple of older guys get messed up by some dipshit youths. There was so much blood coming out of the old guy's head that peanut mouth was tracking it around in footprints, It was a sickening sight but I can't say that it was surprising and I made the decision not to do anything as the old guys were still conscious and managed to get their guards up shortly after the stomping started so I backed off and just waited for the guards to finally step in, it was a bit like waiting for the police when you actually need them.

Chapter 7
Reasoning and Logic

Some guys in this line of work are aware of a sort of, I won't say mutual respect, just understanding between detectives, the real ones, and guys like me, to an extent you begin to appreciate one and other. Right at this very moment some cop is reading this screaming "Bullshit" the reason he did that is he's not a real cop just a wood duck or a drone. The real ones appreciate the fact that guys like me will actually go out of their way to avoid hurting anyone and genuinely have compassion for fellow humans. This may sound ludicrous given my history and I don't blame you if you are sceptical, but I can honestly say I've never hurt another human being other than for reasons of self-defence or to protect someone else. This brings me to my next point, I don't have any ill will towards any officers not even the ones who stood on my neck and kicked me in the ribs and face until I thought I would die. Which is also another reason I want to do my part for those of us who've lost someone with the crime victims fund, also my sincere apologies to those who find my profanity and derogatory language offensive, this is merely to punctuate the narrative and give you a feel for my perspective, and I really do want to stress the reality of crime and although some of the later chapters may glamorize the life a bit I think the first few, particularly 'solitary confinement' should serve as a great deterrent. What most people either don't know, or like me try not to think about is the fact that at any given moment, possibly in human history, there's always someone being persecuted or suffering needlessly, usually there's millions of people suffering needlessly. Obviously, what I've just described is open to fairly broad interpretation but specifically I'm referring to detention and correctional facilities, jails. The reason I'm bringing this up is whilst I did my time I met at least ten guys I knew really didn't belong there, one that I often think of is Seamus, Seamus was a really normal Aussie bloke, despite the name, who was a tradie (tradesman) and up until about a week before I met him had led a fairly normal life - wife, kids, mortgage lots of friends and extended family. Seamus had been heading home from work one day in his commodore when he was involved in an accident, he wasn't at fault but there was a fatality in the other vehicle. This probably sounds like a case of 'so what' well the reason Seamus was now stuck in Hell on earth was that his registration had expired and his renewal had been sent out to the wrong address which meant his vehicle was on the road illegally and he wasn't insured, not even for third party which is what was needed to cover the loss of life and thanks to our great nation's bureaucracy Seamus was looking at six to ten years. If that wasn't enough his misses who as it turns out was banging his boss had left him, taking the kids and defaulting on their home loan which was repossessed by their bank all while he was imprisoned. I have a lot of time for Seamus and eventually when I was back in a different worker's unit, we spent a lot of time playing chess, out of about 55 or so games I only managed to beat Seamus once or twice and I suspect he let me win, not that I'm not good at it it's just that he was freakin awesome! I couldn't blame anyone for guessing that maybe Seamus was in there for an entirely different reason and that perhaps he wasn't as innocent as I claim, but he never volunteered any of this information it was only after many games of chess and some level of trust that he'd confided in me when asked, also he showed me the paper work which would obviously be impossible to fake given the fact that in this particular jail there was no access to computers or printers.

Like I said Seamus was only one of at least ten, and I spent most of my time avoiding people so there must've been plenty. Having said that the overwhelming majority of inmates, like yours truly, were right where they needed to be.

I did however feel really bad for a lot of the young guys in there, who more often than not were homeless and basically had to steal to stay vertical. What a fucked-up introduction to adult life. I found myself feeling less sorry for them when they constantly played freakin rap at full volume, idiots. So many white guys in there who wish they were black and so many black guys in there who wish they were white. But you learn to appreciate the funny side of a lot of this, like young guys who have it in their heads that they're "Gangsta" and act and talk like 50 cent, pfft yeah hours of fun. Then you get guys who are total 'jail heads' in and out all their lives don't know anything else covered in career limiting tatts and yet they still wear fluorescent yellow Nike basketball shoes like a seven year old, adorable.

So I suppose I should bring you up to speed on the lingo, inside the screws insist you refer to the males as 'chief' and the female staff as 'miss' a cigarette is a 'bunga' or a 'pickle'

Champion= cock sucker

China= Mate (rhyming slang ie: China plate or mate) cell= churchie, lighter= jettie, idiot= mort,

chatty= dirty, stretch= sentence duration,

dog= the worst insult you can ever use inside only say this if you are prepared to get very bloody, hang out of = sex

chin = bash

So if you hear someone say "I'm going to chin you and hang out of you you dog!" there's a good chance you're in for a rough night.

Note; There are a lot more terms that are not listed here and general rhyming slang is used frequently too.

Chapter 8
Good Times

This is one of those times that might come along in the lives of the few whom have experienced success in my odd choice of careers, in this case 'epic' success!

This job was flawless, located in another part of Australia I'd cased this target in my usual fashion, solo, intending only to consider the prospect of a heist. When I got there I found very lax security and very low staff morale. The mind-set of the workers is important, it tells you a lot about the management and makes me feel better about my work. Plus it makes it infinitely easier to purchase safe combinations and build a profile for the job.

After frequenting said establishment on and off for a few months I discovered that just before closing the managers would often let people through to the bottle shop after it had been closed. To get there patrons had to actually walk behind the bar and through a staff area to buy their liquor, conveniently this was precisely where the control panel to the alarm system was located.

I'd even seen one of the managers enter his code on closing as we were ushered out, didn't quite get it on that occasion though.

So what I needed to do was wait until closing one night and place a small camera focused on the pad which I would retrieve in the morning, so after a trip to radio shack, dick smith and eventually a small privately owned electronics store I decided to just get a standard point and shoot which would give me about three hours of battery and with a 4gb MSD card about the same in record time.

Next on the agenda was concealment, obviously I couldn't just stick the thing on the wall or I may as well just tell management that I planned on robbing them, sticking to a low budget I simply constructed a shroud made of black paper and believe it or not bought 4 bucks worth of blue tack which I tested for hold time and found would stick basically till the stuff started to rot.

Then about a month later after one of their karaoke nights I waited, till closing with a few stragglers and made my move.

It was easy, I'd rigged the camera in a fashion that enabled me to simply place it in one move and as a bunch of us went through to the bottle shop it was done (should definitely point out that I only handled the camera with the sleeve of my shirt to avoid leaving finger prints and DNA). The next morning I came in while they were opening and asked if they'd found a gold lighter which I thought I may have dropped behind the bar. I had the camera in my pocket before anyone noticed and headed home to get the code.

Next came the safe combo, which I thought would be a real problem given that anyone who really thought about it would be likely to not only 'not' be forthcoming with the combination but possibly likely to alert the police.

So it was a roll of the dice at best, my plan was to maintain anonymity and contact a manager via Email using a dummy address, which I did after picking the least happiest manager whom I'd kind of developed a rappourt with.

In the Email I simply made an offer to buy the combo and just to let him know I was serious asked which bank to chuck $500 in.

Low and behold he replied with his financial details and the next day I Emailed him again after I made a deposit in person wearing a hat and glasses, this time I said if you are willing to give me the combo, "the real one" I will put another $3000 in after I confirm it's real, obviously he had to trust me enough to go ahead so I added I am a man of my word and at the risk of sounding threatening I obviously know where to find you so it's in your interest, PS it's insured and no one will ever be involved least of all hurt PPS you make a wicked martini.

I'd sent the message literally 30 minutes before I heard my phone beep alerting me to an Email on my dummy account, sure enough there were the combination(s), three of them, so the safe actually had three dials, yikes *'must be a biggen'* i remember thinking.

Following this I was really cautious and weary of the establishment and made a point of drinking a lot over the next two weeks while I watched and listened.

I'd Emailed my "buddy" to let him know it would be a couple of months before he would get his 3K so I chucked another $500 in his account, it's funny while I watched him he seemed much happier, maybe because he hated his boss and couldn't wait to see the look on his face when his safe was empty, plus the grand he'd already made for replying to a couple of Emails.

Sitting there over many a beer, I don't drink martinis, I pondered the potential of the job, the place had four bars, a TAB, a restaurant and a bottle-shop and was always packed.

I figured if I hit it on a Sunday before they moved the weekends takings to the bank I'd be looking at 60 to 80K minus the four grand to my buddy and the equipment I'd need it'd be a tidy sum for a few months prep and two to four hours of actual work. So I had the alarm code and the safe combinations now all I needed to do was to pick a night and get inside the place without leaving prints, DNA or my image on any of the many many cameras, the security was lax but a lot better than that of former mentioned venue.

There were a few options for ingress the most appealing to me was the main loading dock which tough as it was, was just a reinforced roller door it'd require a crow bar , not a pinch bar (those little things they call crow bars onTV) a real crow bar is about 6ft long and weights at least 15kgs. Anyway this meant I'd have to carry the bloody thing along with all my other gear, roughly another 20kgs, all the way from my car which I'd leave several blocks from the job, *yay*!

The night before the job I hardly slept as usual but this time for a reason, also I'd been living at a backpackers under an alias to avoid any problems down the track and one of the guys in my room just would not shut the fuck up.

So later that night I'm parked up going over the risks and probability of success constantly repeating a mantra in my head *"You can and will do it" "You can and will do it"*! It seemed like an age before closing time and when it finally rolled around I found my mantra changing to something to the effect of *"I can and will shit myself"!*

I carried that freakin pole and gear bag four blocks sweating and amped for what awaited me, when I was within sight I pulled out the binos and observed the staff finishing up, after waiting twenty minutes I crept the rest of the way fortunately the area was a quite one.

I started my stop watch, next came the reinforced roller door, the main issue was keeping the noise to a minimum. I poked the tip of the crow bar in behind the panel of the roller door and began prising it out of its guide, this was not as easy as I'd hoped! After about 15 minutes of puffing and panting I was about to give up however I'd managed to get just enough of a crack to wedge in a scissor jack from a car that I'd brought along in my gear bag for just this reason. thirty seconds later I was entering the alarm code, immediately after that I practically ran to the office/money room, which I entered with a running front kick just like the cops would at my place if they knew who and where I was back then. By this stage I'm sweating so profusely that I'm practically blind given that I'm wearing a full tracksuit, gloves, balaclava and motor-cross goggles.

So there I was about to enter, the moment of truth, I remember standing in front of this big arse safe hoping I hadn't just broken the law for nothing, did I have the real combinations? Or just some random numbers. I laid out the money bag I'd brought along in front of the safe and went to work on the dials, I'd made a point of memorising the combos just incase but I had it tapped to my arm ready to go. Working the first dial was easy I finished in 20 seconds and heard the tell tale click of the lock falling into place, then the second and finally the third which concerned me as I didn't get it the first time nor the second, bastard! I remember thinking *"That fucking bartender's fucked me, sick prick has given me the first two why not all three!"*

Then I made myself sit down concentrate and breathe I started again and bang it clicked... I think I muttered something out loud like "Oh my fucking gawd!" It was at that moment I wanted to kiss that bloody bartender, I swung the door back and there in front of me sat five shelves of carefully stacked wads and about six bags of coin.

Not wasting a moment I held up the money bag and used

my forearm to slide the loot in which actually didn't all fit, fortunately my cargo pants had big pockets. I remember making a very quick exit and checking my stopwatch, which read 23 minutes and however many seconds.

It's strange but of all the things that happened on that night what I remember most is looking up at the sky as I left and seeing the biggest shooting star I've ever seen and just being overcome with some sense of awe.

A short time after I was in a flash hotel suite counting up what turned out to be a little over 85K, after many a celebratory drink from the minibar in the suites hot tub I decided to head home for a while and spend some time with my folks.

Oh and being a man of my word I Emailed my buddy and told him his money would be in in the morning but given that I didn't want him being a suspect it would be in four separate increments over two weeks and that each increment would be a grand seeing as I was so grateful for a job well done! He was happy and I was wrapped, 5K to Mr Bartender and 81K to yours truly.

Chapter 9
Hindsight is 20-20

I spent many nights laying in my bed analysing and sort of reverse engineering the bungled job. It was clear what could've been done to avoid detection and capture with the job as it stood, even if girly man had ID'd my voice (which he couldn't have done if i'd done a better job at an accent, or better yet avoided talking altogether). All I had to have done was put the loot somewhere safe and changed my car, making sure BA had done the same. But an after thought occurred to me, during my planning for the heist I had considered going solo and using Ketamine as a tranqualliser which I could obtain from a mate who was a veternarian in town.

Simply followed girly man home and using a hired van with alternate rego plates, secured him and obtained his keys and vault combo, for this last part i'd probably need some sodium pentathol (truth agent) which isn't as hard to come by as one would think, at which point I would don a club uniform and glasses, fake mo and just walk in and help myself to 120k. This would've still been a violation of my 'no third parties' rule and was probably worse than just pretending to be armed as it involved druging someone with a hyperdermic needle, which by the way you can actually kill someone with given that they may have an allergic reaction or you may administer the incorrect dose.

This being said, on paper this plan had a much higher likelyhood for success, only involved one count of deprevation of liberty (not six) and had twice the booty to boot. Then somewhere amidst the blur of solitary another thought occurred to me- not ever pulling the fucking job in the first place! I (we) knew it was wrong and hated the fact that there were people involved and as much as I'd like to believe I knew better I think BA felt even worse than I did for perhaps scarring the shit out of those staff.

Don't get me wrong I hate myself for going through with it but I have to admit I don't feel the slightest bit ashamed of using girly man! He is a liar and a manipulator and without going into details he did a real good job of making us seem much worse than we actually were and making himself out to be a hero, despite the fact that he left the girls to fend for themselves that night like the totally gutless wonder he is. In retrospect I should've just kicked the shit out of him, I usually deplore violence just so you know but anyone who hasn't lived in a bubble knows sometimes it's a necessary evil.

All of this frustration aside it didn't help that I was surrounded by dimwitts all to eager to tell me that I should have used a real gun and executed girly man and or any cops that got in the way, mmmm yeah geniuses right?

Whilst inside there were a few goings on in the media to

the effect of 'Police officer slain in bungled robbery' which really made me ill. At one point we even had one of these nutters come in to our prison to await trial and all the dickheads were actually cheering him. When this issue came up at dinner one night I remember distinctly having a chat with a young guy I'd assumed wasn't a total retard until now. He said " I reckon he did the right thing, nearly got away too!" to which I responded, "Are you fucking nuts?"

Kid- "Why? What would you do? Use your cap gun?"

Me-"I'm not dumb enough to put innocent people at risk in the first place halfwitt!"

Kid- "But what if it's you or them?"

Me- "It's only like that if you make it that way, all he had to do was put the gun on the ground and his hands in the air!"

Kid- "He'd still be in here!"

Me- "Yeah but he wouldn't die in here like he will now!"

Kid- "oh yeah I spose"

Me- "And surely even you are aware that that officer had a wife and kids? What about his poor bloody kids? What did they do to deserve this?"

In truth, before, during and after my stay in these correctional centres and the job I often think that I shouldn't have done it at all even with a fool-proof plan and even if I had pulled it off scot free I don't think it ever would've sat right with me. I mean before I got into this life I'd worked in positions of trust and cash handling and if the tills were out by a few bucks you'd see me amend them with my own cash. I prided myself on always doing the right thing and trying to help others, which I still do I just think that I've stigmatised myself and am very aware of it at all times now. Never ceases to amaze me the amount of people inside and out that blame everyone but themselves, people that are just consumed by hatred and are controlled by their emotions. Not going to preach to you and pretend that I'm some sort of enlightened being with all the answers but I do know I've learned a lot about myself and about the way others perceive me to be.

I was a prolific reader before my incarceration but inside it was like breathing, it's all I did, except for work, play chess and eventually study. One thing I found however was that there was a distinct lack of decent reading material inside, and generally the genres seemed to centre around the morbid, though if you walk into most bookstores these days the true-crime section is always the biggest and streaming sites seem to add a new Murdermentary, that's what I call series about murders and forensics, every day. What I was really craving was access to self help lifestyle type books like those by Tony Robbins or James A. King, I really think if there was a business section in the prison with the likes of Scott O'neill, Robert Kiyosaki and others then there would be a higher likelihood for positive change among the prisoners but during my time here I simply had to channel this type of thinking internally and look for the good amongst the bad.

It's very comical to me that a so called close friend of mine that I've known since we were four to five years old has completely excommunicated me and from what I hear keeps telling others to do the same, what's funny is that when we were in high school and probably now even he was a certified kleptomaniac, never paid for anything he could steal and spent most of his time ripping of one of our mates Dad's who owned a news agency, some friend right? To top that off he joined, well tried to join, the fire brigade and he is responsible for starting numerous fires around our town a couple of which caused serious damage to people's property as he, we suspect, is a pyromaniac too. But apparently he's too good to associate with someone who steals insured cash. What a laugh!

Chapter 10
Exploits of Other Inmates

Possibly the most common charge I came across inside was fraud. Which to me is a bad one as it makes the future of the offender very very difficult. When someone is convicted of this charge it is actually mandatory for said offender to openly disclose this fact to any potential employers and also to others in some instances too I believe.

One such offender I met had approached me with a job offer after learning of my studies and my past. We'll call him 'Rick', Rick was in for the illegal appropriation of no less than $750,000 when in actual fact, according to Rick, it was considerably more.

He had basically set up fraudulent websites and obtained peoples credit card details and just purchased a bunch of high end items to then on sell to generate an income. This is a fairly common set up but eventually everyone comes undone. Again this sort of thing does not appeal to me as it often has real repercussions for real people though credit-card fraud is usually covered by insurance for the card holder. Rick's proposal was a bit more technical and had a much higher probability for success, I don't think that by putting the broad strokes in writing I am putting him in any danger as it's such a sneaky idea I think that even if I was to tell the police directly, not that I ever would obviously, they still wouldn't be able to get him. His idea is fairly simple but involves a lot of technical aptitude, he wants a group of guys posing as contractors, who in effect are contractors, to drive all over major cities using vans provided by him, looking like technicians accessing phone service junctions, those things that look like big torpedoes sticking out of the ground, then the guys use the junctions to send a few hundred free out going calls, per day, to homes who are actually charged a small flag fall which goes to a dummy company set up by Rick. This may sound terrible to some people but at the end of the day it's just a couple of bucks each and if you are really upset by this then you must want to kill the service providers over here who often blatantly overcharge, charge for calls that were never made and just provide a crap service all round.

Rick's plan was to eventually have ten guys making 1000 calls each per day for him, so yeah 20K a day minus the pay for said guys 2-300 each, not bad if you can live with the moral dilemma and avoid the authorities.

Rick and I both had the privilege of meeting a man whom had defrauded the Australian government of 44 million dollars ,I've massaged that number slightly down as his exploits are searchable online, this guy did it all using paper work and bearer bonds which he had deposited in an account in Hong Kong which has banking laws protecting it and given that the authorities can only hold him for so long eventually he will ,in theory, rendezvous with his loot and live happily ever after, though I fear that if he is unwilling to return the money he is still technically breaking more laws and/or the conditions of his potential parole. Either way I'm pretty sure he wishes he had skipped the country a tad earlier. Rick and this guy along with my friend Seamus and a few others represented the nicer side of the prison population. As previously mentioned I had encountered murderers, rapists, cannibals, paedophiles, arsonists and even a few guys in there for torture, for some reason the guys I met that were in for torture were often proud of that fact and thought of the charge kind of like a badge of honour, sickos.

But about midway through my sentence I found myself paying more attention to the crimes reported in the paper than usual as it was often very relative to the people around me and especially the new guys coming in.

One such case involved a guy that at first glance was good looking, intelligent and pretty funny too. He'd been in our unit for about two weeks when he started having dramas with some of the other inmates, I made a point of never asking guys why they were in unless they'd asked me or we'd known each other a while, whereas this guy had, apparently, made a point of asking everyone and willingly told them that he was in for killing and dismembering his girlfriend. At first, I didn't believe it and gave him the benefit of the doubt until one afternoon I was talking to him near his cell and saw a newspaper clipping of an article about the whole thing with his picture right there stuck on his wall like a bloody trophy, even more disturbing was a sort of shrine he'd made of his girlfriend right next to the article with little love hearts all over it, kooku kooku!

I found a copy of the article at the library and had to read it out of morbid curiosity and shock, according to the article his girlfriend's corpse had been discovered in a wheelie bin outside her house, and he'd killed her with the help of his other girlfriend, makes you wonder what she thought about this? I mean surely the prospect of the same fate had occurred to her?

Any way I made a point of having as little to do with this guy as possible, the last time we spoke he was telling me how he and a female prisoner, convicted of killing her boyfriend, were now pen pals, I wonder if their offspring would have a propensity to be homicidal.

I wish I could say that that was one of the worst cases I'd heard of but in reality, it's probably somewhere in the middle.

I was shocked to learn of an incident involving a guy that I'd met inside, I only learned of the real reason he was sentenced after my release which in hindsight was probably a good thing. I knew he'd been charged with assault, which isn't a big deal, depending on the circumstances, what I didn't know was that in addition to that charge he was charged with malicious wounding, grievous bodily harm and attempted murder. Again, this may not sound too bad to some people, I mean if it was in self-defence, but it wasn't. What had actually happened is he had gotten into an altercation with another motorist while in a stolen car and decided the best way to deal with this guy, who had gotten out of his car, was to take a tyre iron to his children in the back seat. The sick prick had actually brutalised these little children in a fit of road rage with a length of heavy metal. One of which was nearly killed and will never be the same again thanks to the head injuries inflicted by this coward.

Chapter 11
Catch and Release

Upon release from a correctional centre aside from the initial overwhelming relief and short lived euphoria that you feel you'll be suddenly very aware of your somewhat limited rights as a so called free man. Depending on your classification (level of risk to re-offend) you will have to report to a parole officer about once a month and provide urine samples and information relative to your situation following release. This may not sound like a big deal, and often isn't, however most of the guys that get out aren't as lucky as me and don't have a loving and supportive family willing to offer help until they get back on their feet, so they find themselves in a halfway house surrounded by guys that they've served time with and who are very likely to be a bad influence on said parolee. This makes it extremely hard for ex-cons to assimilate back into the workforce and society, in addition to being housed with other parolees they are targeted by drug dealers as an easy sale, it doesn't take a marketing genius to realise former drug users fresh out of prison will pay whatever they can to get a fix or temporary escape from the depressing reality that is parole.

None of these conditions affected me fortunately, what was a major pain in the arse however was the fact that I had a mandatory dry ban (no alcohol) imposed on me and that no matter how many letters I wrote or how well I did or the fact that my offenses had nothing to do with alcohol, they just didn't care. So at this point I'd like to state the obvious and that is the fact that I drank my brains out quite often and also frequented licensed establishments to boot, casinos, bars and restaurants too. It is utterly laughable that these idiots would, and in fact do, send people back to prison for simply enjoying a quiet drink at home or being caught in a night club while on parole, clearly this mind-set has nothing to do with rehabilitation. Although the afore-mentioned problems are quite bad the worst of it was actually policies and procedures for new address approval, this is where the public service stigma really gets its credit. In this particular part of Australia the Parole Board can take up to twenty one days to approve a dwelling for you to take up residence 'twenty one' days! (And I'm told it's even longer in other states) Yeah so all realistic hope of acquiring an actual safe and secure place to live without breaking the law is non-existent. If you're reading this prior to release or are currently looking for a place, just move and then apply keeping a low profile until you receive approval, or better yet don't bother telling them at all because if this is how they treat us and you have kept your nose clean simply having a decent lawyer and keeping a log of all this BS and how impossible it makes life will keep you out of any sanction, seriously what a bunch of wankers! If you plan on getting approval to live in a share-house forget it as you have to not only disclose your history to the housemates but provide contacts for your officer to confirm this with them and let's face it most of us wouldn't want to live with a crim if we could help it and I'd be wary of anyone who would. Job prospects are often affected by your history, as mentioned earlier however there is only one charge, other than the really serious ones, where you have to in fact disclose said charge. This fact is lost on a lot of companies and individuals however and they will quite often write things in their applications like, 'Have you/ or do you live with anyone whom has been charged with committing an offense in the last ten years?' and they also write crap like 'will you pass a background check (which our company will issue upon successful application?' Fortunately in Australia we have something known as the 'Privacy Act' which is both State and Federal Law and thankfully works to keep our business protected and states that other than an investigating officer with specific clearance relative to an investigation and/or a warrant, 'you' and you alone are the only person in this country who can access your criminal history and when you actually are applying for a position that in fact does require real background checks what you are required to do is provide what's known as a police clearance. These are only needed when applying to work for the Australian government, with children or when applying for a high trust/high risk position at a bank or a gold mine etc. I had been out for all of about a month when a friend of my sister's was around and offered to help get me a job which turned out to be a waste of time as this twit just couldn't get his head around the fact that not only was I not required to tell his company about my history but it had nothing to do with him in the first place. The dimwit just kept saying 'I gotta tell em mate otherwise I'm liable you know?' Liable? Liable for fucking what? Idiot, and who's to say you should know about it in the first place, Christ some people are dumb! Anyway despite being eternally grateful for the help my sister had afforded me after my mishap I politely informed her that if that guy was around much it would inevitably end with him taking a trip to hospital. Knowing that I'd never say this unless I meant it she made arrangements that negated his presence in the future. So in short when a company or business says to you that they need to know your criminal past you should know this is a bluff, they have no right, fortunately, in this country to demand this information, unless of course you did time for fraud or something really bad. I must say that I have and continue to work in roles where they have actually played this card, and I say 'fuck em!' Besides following extensive chats with both my solicitor and my parole officers they are all adamant that you are within your rights to say 'no'. Some would argue that this is deceitful and that you are obliged to be truthful or refuse to answer which is as good as an admission of guilt. To these people I say they don't have the right to ask in the first place so again 'fuck em!'

Chapter 12
Relationships

It was quite a while after I got out before I started dating again, just in dribs and drabs at first. I had one relationship with a young woman that was just purely sexual as it turns out. I'd like to mention that I told her about my past almost as soon as things got semi-serious and she was okay with it, of course if she'd learned of my exploits through other sources as opposed to from the horse's mouth it would have been very hard for her to trust me because the papers and article excerpts online didn't paint a terribly flattering picture as you can imagine. Not long after that fling fizzled out I found myself using online dating sites, well 'one' to be exact, and low and behold the first woman I landed was a forensic police officer. Needless to say I avoided mentioning my former life entirely with this one, and it wasn't long before we'd crossed a line that possibly obligated me to be more forthcoming with my history.

Fortunately for me she wasn't that keen to make anything serious out of what we had anyway so problem solved. In the meantime my mates constantly made references to a certain NWA track with the acronym FTP! Yeah they thought it was hilarious, though I'm sure officer 'what's her name' wouldn't think it was so funny. The dating game continued until I met a chick that I liked straight away and seemed, unbelievably, to be as keen on me as I was her. We hung out as often as possible and it wasn't long before I dropped the bomb surrounding my criminal past. She was more surprised than concerned as she just couldn't picture me being involved in something like that, come to think of it neither can I for that matter, again it went against my principles. Things were going great with this girl it even got to the stage where we were basically sharing the nights between our respective houses and considering moving in together. One thing that had always concerned me regarding the disclosure issue is that I'd be totally gutted if any one used it as a weapon in the event of an argument, fortunately my lovely lady friend never did. An issue that had been raised however was the fact that my girl liked to travel and obviously until my parole conditions changed, which wasn't due to come into effect for another four years, we couldn't do this together unless I intended not to return. Before I met her I had seriously considered joining the French Foreign Legion for just this reason. Unfortunately as with all my previous relationships this one was about to end because of the same issue, locality, every single semi-serious girlfriend I've had has been lost because of a situation where one of us moved to the other side of the country or has been offered a dream job on the other side of the country, either that or she's a psycho! On the plus side this freed up a lot of time to put some hours in on my book and also freed up a lot of cash, don't get me wrong I believe in romancing your woman and spoiling her but it can get really expensive really fast, of course it's all worth it for the right girl and should you end up living together it becomes cost effective anyway. None of this mattered now.

After parting ways with my significant other I didn't really have anything serious for a long while, dribs and drabs again, and then I started to find that it became easy to attract women that wanted to try and maintain a serious relationship with me. One such woman was very dear to me and most would think of her as exotic, just my type. We were serious enough to move in and tough it out for the best part of a year, unfortunately it seems she had more emotional issues than I did, and despite my best efforts to help, or at least find help, she just seemed to get worse. One of the aspects of this relationship that made it all the more difficult was that fact that this one did actually use my past as a means of wounding me, and this hurt me more than she could ever know. I'm not going to claim to be the perfect gentleman though I do know I would never use violence against women but this one would work herself into a state of hysteria and get quite physical with me, throwing things and punching me. I have to say when this happens I get more than a little scared not for myself but for what may lay ahead for women with this mentality, one time she got so bad that in a moment of weakness I decided restraining her was a good idea, big mistake, she thrashed around punching and clawing so bad that she'd not only bloodied my nose but scratched her face a little. My worst fears were coming alive when she said she would call the police and tell them I did this to her, which I guess was technically not a lie. Eventually we made a mutual decision to end it.

The flat we shared belonged to a very nice elderly

eastern European woman whom I'd noticed had an incredibly hot niece, I should mention I did my best not to notice this while I was committed to my ex. However as we'd broken up I couldn't justify paying the exorbitant rent on my own so when the day came to leave my former landlord suggested I give her niece a call and gave me her number, I could've done a happy dance right there and then.

Things started off great as we both loved bikes and cars and the beach I'd take her for rides on my Ducati and before we knew it she was spending many nights at my new place with me. I was reluctant at first to put too much faith in any hope of the relationship lasting as she was only 22 and from a part of the world not known for monogamy or compassion, sorry if this offends you but stereo types exist for a reason, however I gave her the benefit of the doubt and we made plans for a sea-change to a very popular tourist mecca in Eastern Australia, given my past relationship disasters I made a point of moving with this one as I didn't want to have any more 'what ifs' on my mind. Friends and family said I was nuts as I was walking away from a high paying job to risk it all for 'some barbie doll' as they called her. I'd immediately defend her to them saying 'She's not like that, she's different.' Never totally believing it, as it turns out I was totally blind in love with this girl as she confided that even while we'd been dating she had maintained a relationship for a while stating 'but I'm glad you didn't give up and I want *you* now' like this was some sort of gift from her for which I should feel privileged. Then when we got to our new home and eventually I started running out of money that's when her lack of care got really obvious, she'd spend long periods out of reach never answering her phone while she was with her new male friend, also from the same eastern bloc country, one night she said we had to end it as she had too many missed calls from me and that I loved her too much. *Fuck me! Is that a thing?*

It was incredibly hard to just get over this whole predicament, added to this I was now not only broke but my various accounts were overdrawn which meant I had to live in my car, occasionally I'd hear from what's her face, and the shameless nature of her admissions is what led me to include some account of her bullshit here. Not only had she left me to live in my car, after I'd payed thousands of dollars for her college fees and hundreds of dollars for dental, medical and fuel, food and accommodation but what's her face, had no problem telling me that she was now sharing a bed with this guy and that while we had been dating she'd often shared a bed with male friends. If that wasn't a kick in the balls I'd only just finished trying to take the high road saying- 'don't worry about the money, it's all good, we're family' this fruit loop had literally only known this guy for two weeks and was quite content to share a bed with him 'and' share the rent for Christ's sakes, she never contributed a dollar to our entire spending.

I'm sure that I'm not the only one when faced with a dilemma like this would have a strong inclination to become extremely violent with the other male in this story, although it would be counterproductive given that at this point I was still serving parole and that one couldn't really blame him for the situation any way. That being said it took great composure and much self-counselling to refrain from just doing some very, very, nasty stuff to this guy.

Friends oblivious to my parole situation would ask, 'Why don't you belt this guy?' and friends that knew would actually offer their services, one really good friend that has known me since I had a clean record and was actually in town when my offence happened has a boyfriend that is affiliated with a known outlaw motorcycle gang situated right in the town in question, and when he heard of my troubles I basically had to ensure he didn't find out who and where these people were as he was set on belting the pair of them, or at least belting the bloke to the point where neither of them would consider contacting the police, to his credit his heart was in the right place.

Earlier I mentioned the fact that I found myself crying only once during my incarceration and with the exception of being reunited with my little sister for the first time in eight years understandably making me a bit glassy eyed that was completely true. However following this last break up I swear I must have been dehydrated with the amount of balling I did, apologies if this doesn't gel well with the whole true crime genre but truth is I am very human and was utterly devastated by this girl to the point where it was socially crippling. Sure I could pretend to be all hard and indifferent or I could even be the guy that doesn't care, but why be someone who will never know love for fear of feeling. Often I've been super tempted to try and be the jerk that has no emotional investment with females and simply lurches from lay to lay, these wankers appear to be the happiest of all. Though I'm just not wired that way, honestly even when I've found myself in the closing stages of a relationship that I couldn't get totally into and even when there were options and real offers elsewhere that is something I could never do. At the risk of flogging a dead horse, I am ever aware that what I did to land myself in trouble with the authorities was wrong and truly a bad move. Though to put things into perspective, mostly for female readers, we never hurt nor risked harm to others the entire time, all 8-9 minutes of it and while it was a despicable act, I can't fathom how one can pretend to care for someone or even actually care for someone, let them put their heart and soul on the line only to gut them like a fish with infidelity or a humiliating break up. I know without a shadow of a doubt that I was suffering more after that break up than I ever did in prison or as a result of the various physical traumas I've suffered over the years, to this you may say well if she doesn't want you, she doesn't want you! While this is true, she sure made the most of someone she didn't want whilst it was convenient.

In any event I eventually learned to forgive her and move on, which if I'm being honest was actually a huge relief and weight off my shoulders.

Chapter 13
Interstate

Following a decision to be closer to my family I applied to move from the state I was serving my parole in at the time, and Holy Crap, talk about a cluster fuck.

Initially I was told by my officer, blonde very blonde, that upon successful application I'd be notified within 2 weeks and given that my family was there and that I had only ever had one charge in one state/territory it was a no brainer. Any way me being me wanting to do right by my employer and landlord gave notice and prepared to move. I should also mention that the officer told me that in the event that the approval took longer she'd simply replenish temporary passes, holiday passes, till it went through.

I should have known from the start! Having begun the application in November and leaving my job and my house I was told that the application had been put into review status, to which I asked the obvious, what does that mean for me time wise?

Blondie- 'Well it could be a while now!'

'Oh fucking great!' I'm thinking.

When the holiday application came through after three weeks of living in my car with my dog and all my worldly possessions like a bum I drove 1,100kms to my Dad's house and following a nice six days of relaxation was informed by Blondie that they actually couldn't replenish the temporary passes and that I'd have to come back!

'What in the fuck shit fuck are you fucking kidding me you fucking retarded public servant?'

Just great! So there I am dirt poor, no job and nowhere to stay as I've worn out my welcome with my sister and would prefer not to bother her if possible any way using my only option- a bloody half way house.

Awaiting a decision from the other states Parole Board- which as it turns out took another three fucking months!

Just what I needed, yeah being surrounded by crims in the city add to that the fact that they have access to drugs and weapons in this environment and it's a pretty shit-house way to live.

What you find there is a lot of the poor bastards trapped in this situation end up living on park benches anyway just as a means to escape the sort of pricks you get stuck with in these places. I tried to distance myself from the other guys in there but you invariably end up making a few friends and as one would expect tend to gravitate towards likeminded people. One of the guys I met was a former cook in the

ADF, Australian Defence Force, with a unit that I actually applied for back when I was eligible for service and way into my rock climbing and diving etcetera.

I'd met a guy years earlier through a mutual friend whilst climbing that was fairly high up in the fourth Royal Australian Regiment or 4RAR for short, 4RAR is a fulltime unit based in Holsworthy Sydney and aside from the SASR is the only fulltime Special Forces unit and its members are trained as Commandos. Naturally, back then in my climbing days, I immediately took an interest in my new friend's job and was keen to find out more so not long after meeting this mysterious guy I found myself at the ADF's recruitment centre applying for the role of Commando.

I wouldn't blame you for thinking that it's a tad grandiose to assume I even have a chance of getting through the programme but at the time I was ridiculously fit, training for and competing in triathlon, rock climbing, actually running 42 Ks just to see how I'd do, riding 27Ks to and from a physically demanding job each day and then training on top of that, plus I'd always had an interest in the nature of that job and new more than most.

In any case I obviously didn't get through the selection, in fact I didn't start as following my letter of job offer I almost broke my ankle while training for said selection and by the time another intake rolled around I'd already chased opportunity in the Mines of Western Australia. Despite all this I had an instant friendship with my new mate KP, the former 4RAR cook.

KP had lived an interesting life at every stage and from what I would later learn his stint with the Commandos probably seemed to him like a bit of a holiday in terms of tempo and stress levels. He's probably the only reason I didn't go completely mental while stuck in that shit hole of a place as he was always good for a yarn and a practical joke plus despite being unemployed and homeless was in fact extremely enterprising. I don't think it'd bother KP for me to tell you that the reason he'd found himself in this predicament was he'd had a bit of an altercation with some Police Officers, I'd tell you that they were using excessive force but in this particular part of Australia I don't think they know any other way, irrespective of their methods it took five of them to eventually get him into a paddy wagon according to some of the staff at the hole where this happened.

One thing that struck me when I was hanging around with my mate was after a while I began noticing similarly dressed folks paying just a little too much attention KP and even taking photos and not long thereafter he said to me 'You might think I'm being paranoid, but I'm actually under surveillance presently'.

'No shit' - I thought. 'Are you part of an investigation?'

KP- 'Not that I'm aware of, I'm actually staying well clear of anything real dodgy!'

KP actually suffers from PTSD though it actually has

nothing to do with the military and everything to do with some shady characters and the boot of a car one scary night way back in the day when KP was involved in something way less honourable than serving with the commandos.

Without going into too much detail it was basically a case of mistaken identity and given that I don't know the facts or even anyone's version of the facts I'd only be speculating as to exactly what happened but from what I have been told if it was anyone but KP they wouldn't be here to tell the story.

Any way three fucking months later it was time to say adios to my friends and head interstate, again. This all took place not long after the Abbott government was installed, I have to say that as I refuse to believe the Australian public were dumb enough to give the majority to that wanker, and what I found in this new state (you'll have to guess which one) is that their probation & parole policy demands that you see these muppets every single week, sometimes twice in the same week I would find!

'Are you fucking kidding me?'

My case officer, actually a really nice lady though thick as a hammer, said that every two weeks may be possible in a month so after a month hooray we did go to every second week, however following a holiday, at the tax payers expense, she gets back and tells me- 'No mate it's always been every week it's just as I was away!'

'What the fuck?'

Then add to that horror, after a few months of these dreaded visits to this miserable joint she tells me the maximum threshold for the frequency of visits is now every four weeks, not eight not six but fucking four! Courtesy of the Liberals, the first time I met this woman she was telling me if things go well I could comply with a simple phone call. I don't care what your tolerance policy on crime is or who you are, if you can't see how this sort of BS is detrimental to so called rehabilitation then I suggest you get someone nearby come and help explain the basic concepts in this book along with the big words as you are just plain daft.

Speaking of daft, my parole officer loved to explain this 'crackdown' on parole conditions by explaining that thanks to the poor handling of a high profile murder/rape case in Melbourne this has happened, which basically means that because some useless fat idiot like her in Victoria is so lazy and dumb and let a three times convicted serial rapist just ignore his parole conditions and offended again the rest of us have to be fucked over. She also had this wonderful way of explaining that fact as if I was a rapist and/or a murderer and she spoke to me as if I were a five year old child which was entertaining as most five year olds I've conversed with are far more switched on.

In any case I didn't really care too much what she thought and simply moved into my own place almost immediately and kept to myself, all the while letting her and the rest of the geniuses at the parole office think that I still resided at my Dad's house, "Yeah totally! Hmm let's see? I'm a thirty five year old parolee on the work force, think I'll just stay at my Dad's house for two years!"

During my time on parole I must note that despite not being totally forthright with my officers I only received one actual warning thanks to the above mentioned officers incompetence entirely I might add, and the situation unfolded as follows.

I arrived to see this idiot at the scheduled meeting and even apologised to her as I'd missed my first ever appointment the week prior due to a work commitment, things were going fairly standardly and it seemed as if we were getting on well when she stated that I need to make my GP information, including contact details, available ASAP.

To which I responded politely with- 'I'm happy to help though I don't believe it's mandatory as I'm not on a treatment order'.

The imbecile immediately became irate and threatened my liberty for simply attempting to stand up for my rights, all the while talking to me in the tone and guise of a disinterested four year old. It was at this point I said- 'Please don't talk to me in that tone as you're agitating me!'

It's important to remember these dickheads, some of them, have a god complex and love to threaten you and take away what little rights you have and make your life miserable though if you even hint at the prospect of standing up for your freedom they will take it upon themselves to make all manner of claims against you, and in this state they don't monitor/record your interviews at all, which is really daft and means it's your word against theirs.

Any way following what happened next I began recording all meetings myself.

Following my off the cuff comment about the nature of my order and then using the word 'agitating' she promptly stood and ordered me to leave.

Approximately twenty-five minutes later I received a call from her team leader- a slightly less stupid though equally if not more ball busting, man hating bureaucrat named after a type of cheese, so for the purpose of the book we shall refer to her as Blue Vein.

So any way the first words out of Blue Vein's mouth were 'Mitch we're breaching you!' This initially sounded like a misguided exaggeration as a means to scare me as I'd left the office on bad terms and figured she'd be reasonable, though this dim wit was actually dead serious and when I asked why? She stated that I had failed to provide the requested Dr's info for approximately nine months,

'What in the Fuck?'

I had literally only just been informed of this situation not thirty minutes earlier! Apparently this fat idiot, my parole officer, had kept notes to the effect that she had been continually reminding me of this situation since day dot. Which obviously meant either she was saving this as ammunition to ruin my life should she feel like it, meaning I hadn't given her enough credit for conniving potential. Or the more likely reason she had a simple tick and flick system, government employees are so lazy, and it appeared on her notes though she had never actually done her job at all.

In any case this now meant I had to take even more time off work running around paying to see Doctors for no actual benefit to me and following a long winded sycophantic letter to the Parole Board would receive a warning.

Oh great, because it's not as if I wasn't putting up with enough BS from these monkeys in the first place. So if you find yourself wondering how your tax dollars are being spent to "rehabilitate" offenders you may find it interesting to know that the non- serious offenders (Yes I know what I did was pretty bad) are being pushed to the point of breaking and given every reason not to want and be a good citizen.

You may be reading this and still thinking, what is this guy on about? Well had I been actually breached by these two dipshits I would have promptly been arrested and remanded in custody for twenty eight days, So I'd loose my job, my apartment, my girlfriend potentially and if you're as daft as these two cretins and think I'd simply be released as a frightened good little boy who believed that he was in there through his own doing and that there'd be no reason for these two to be concerned, think again.

I despise violence against women and have put myself in harm's way to protect women, be they right or wrong however when I received that call from Blue Vein all manner of violent urges began rising in my blood and although I would never harm them directly, maybe just belt the absolute shit out of their partners, I have to say that had I been breached which was their intention any and all consequences would have been created solely and certainly by them and them alone. Anyone whether clean skinned or convicted has to appreciate that when a person's liberty and basic rights are threatened 'especially' through no doing of their own they are going to be extremely pissed off!

Looking back on this years later, I still wouldn't have elicited any direct violence against these idiots, though I would have organised for some serious mind fucking, ie- stealing their E-tag, toll way transponder, and fixing it to a city bus to rack up thousands in bills, using industrial adhesive to glue the doors on their cars shut, basically all manner of cathartic relief to turn a frown upside down.

Chapter 14
Crazy House

In addition to the formerly mentioned living situation in my new state the parole conditions in general meant that I always had to be extra nice to everyone and even when I was being treated unfairly say by a lessor or landlord there wasn't much I could do as in reality I wasn't legally supposed to be there in the first place, one such situation came about shortly after leaving my Dad's place when my loopy landlord began to make things so uncomfortable for myself and my girlfriend that we decided to get out of dodge.

This nutcase hadn't lodged a proper bond with the Rental Tenancy Authority and only accepted cash each week so we knew she was a bit dodgy to begin with, added to that upon arrival there was a note taped to the back of the door stating a rather long list of all the dos and don'ts. The bond was a standard four weeks or $1400 however on the bond receipt she'd written three weeks notice is required upon leaving, in other words this fruitcake thought this was a contract to forfeit my bond as virtually no one can organise the house they want and have it held for three weeks! As mentioned above she'd made it so awkward we wanted out immediately any way.

There are multiple reasons for wanting out of this shitty situation which is strange as I already made a point of always being polite and helpful and this was especially true following my recent brush with the law. I'd spent money improving this woman's apartment, took her garbage in and out each week, helped with her gardening and fixed her gates (at my own expense) only to find her treating my girlfriend, who'd moved in later, with distain and eventually treating both of us like filth. So following a few months of this I came home one day from a particularly long hard day to find she'd had the smoke alarms changed and a few things had been moved without us getting a heads up. As you can imagine she got a "Please explain?" via mobile call as I couldn't stand the sight of her, although I should stress that I was very polite when I asked.

'Do you know that someone was in our apartment today Marge?' To which she replied- 'Yes I had the smoke alarms changed.'

'Um well we didn't know anyone was coming.'

And this next part is what made the decision to leave ASAP easy

'I don't need to tell you Mitch, you're only renting you don't own the apartment!'

As you can imagine this fruit loop intended to use the whole 'I need three weeks notice' bullshit to which I responded with the standard 'I'll go to the tribunal.'

Anyway following a fourteen hour day of moving it got to the stage where I just wanted to get out of there and on the last load of removals, the crucial one, I arrived with a mate to get the lounges only to find the bitch had parked us out and when I asked as politely as anyone could muster she started yelling "stop being aggressive or I'll call the police!" My mate and I both knew the score if that happened! In any other situation I would have called them hours ago to help resolve the bond situation, I know this is not their job however often their presence has a tendency to make people more inclined to cooperate or be reasonable. So, after all this shit the crazy, crazy nut bitch texts- I will be getting the house cleaned professionally, I decided to leave without vacuuming as I was stuffed, and I will also get a quote for the damage to my car. When queried on this subject she claims I scratched her shit-box car with my Ducati one day (yeah totally- I just figured I'd use my pride and joy shiny crotch rocket to scuff up your POS rust bucket) I then received a photo via text showing a mark, not a scratch, about half the size of a 5 cent piece, naturally I figured 'what the hell it couldn't be more than fifty bucks right?' wrong! She organised a quote for an entire bumper removal/respray totalling almost $600.00!

Bearing in mind her car had such badly faded roof paint it looked as if it may not pass registration! This woman truly was warped! I soon found myself less inclined to share the story of my adventures in the nut house, nutcase apartment, as my friends were offering their services in the form of beatings and 'actual' damage to her car etc which I really couldn't let happen. I mean, even if I were still clean skinned and I'd let someone get away with this, which I wouldn't, it wouldn't sit well with me. I deplore violence against women, even if the services rendered were provided by another female like my girlfriend at the time who was a boxer, and I think damaging someone else's property in their absence is cowardly. In reality I feel better not doing anything as I know I am a better person, yes it's cliché, and she is in fact sad and alone and has to create drama in order to feel as though she has a purpose.

It's funny but I am truly starting to believe that my time served has allowed me to develop a bit of calm and tolerance to this sort of treatment, because as infuriating as this was at the time it actually affected my friends and family much more in that they were the ones that wanted some sort of reprisal action taken against this unhinged woman, and the more I think of it the more patience I develop in letting it go.

I know that this lunatic it truly deserving of some bad things following her behaviour, however I would get no satisfaction from being the one to arrange it and I don't even want to waste my time thinking about it let alone involve myself, it really is more gratifying to be able to relieve yourself of a gripe than to get all caught up in one.

Chapter 15
Retrospectively Bad

Often, I wonder what things would have been like if I'd thrown aside my morals and applied myself to a lifestyle entirely about personal gain and didn't care about others. For example by the time I was in year seven I knew about card readers (electronic ones- not nerds in a casino) and how to use them to identify the pin number of someone's bank/credit cards and the like, if I didn't care about others or how I was living my life all I would have had to do was find a way to get my hands on peoples cards and simply withdraw all their cash- credit included, by the way this money would also be insured though I do not/nor ever have I liked the idea of stealing from an individual. Though if I was that way inclined and still wanted to avoid hurting or risking hurting someone, I could find ways around it. Touching on a subject mentioned earlier, lock smithing is a highly technical trade that is ever evolving and a position of trust, that being said I'm a bit reluctant to elaborate on this though I'm sure it's occurred to locksmith's the world over, or anyone that's ever locked themselves out of the house or car you will know just how shockingly easy these guys make it look when they need to get past a lock, if one was inclined and skilled in this trade they would be virtually untouchable, so long as they took precautions to never leave

DNA and avoided contact with third parties. If I had my time again and found myself jaded with society and didn't owe so much to my family, lock smithing and alarm security is where I'd probably find myself, with regard to the alarm side of things I have a good mate who's brother installs security garage doors and makes a mint doing it, I once witnessed him spend all of about 20 seconds scanning and finding the correct frequency to his brother's garage door and making himself a remote about the size of a small watch, to that you might say- 'Well mine's scrambled and security encrypted!', So was his.

You don't have to be a criminal mastermind to see that if someone with these skills goes bad there's not much stopping them from starting a very quick, virtually risk- free turn over simply taking things out of rich people's garages. I'd forgive you for thinking that it's stupid to say that it could be risk free but think for a moment- You're targeting big properties, you don't use a vehicle that 'if' identified leads to you and you just make sure you have the frequency before the score and that no one's there at the time with a man on station (or two if needed) just up the road on a radio waiting to give you the heads up. Add to that the ability to start and take a vehicle (the best ones are usually there) and before you know it you've got a criminal enterprise pumping more coin than a Macca's franchise next to a cop shop!

Another little scheme that came to me, again 'only' the theory, was when I used to work in marketing and was aware that a lot of information is readily accessible through certain means, for example when Australia's electricity and utilities legislation was deregulated and people were given the option of choosing a different provider marketing companies had access to lists of addresses and customers that used certain providers etcetera and given that companies could get this list then Joe Criminal could also get it and of course if Joe Criminal is technically proficient enough he'd know that most people during this time used Bpay or the Internet to balance their bills and exploit this fact. It's quite a bit of work for Joe Criminal for a potentially moderate pay day or heaps of work for a huge pay day and then some.

Business savvy individuals know that in order to register for a biller code account all you need is a company name and a financial institution that uses Bpay along with a successful application for the account to be linked to yours.

Once Joe Criminal has successfully registered a Bpay account the tricky part begins. Getting hold of as many different provider bills as possible and then the information necessary to send out counterfeit electricity bills around the same time as they are due though slightly early to give you a window. You may be aware that in certain suburbs eventually almost all the residents used to begin to receive bills almost in sync as the metres used to be read and received at the same time so it's simple, Joe Criminal has his list and creates his alternate bills with his, not the companies, biller code and to try and make things smoother a very reasonably priced bill stating that customer's bills are coming down in an effort to encourage early bill payment or some other BS to that effect, wow seems like a lot of effort that ultimately looks very likely to land Joe Criminal where he belongs?, however let's say the average bill is a quarterly for around $200.00 and that he targets a couple of rich suburbs, gets all the angles right and doesn't alert anyone to his con ahead of time and the suburbs have 5,000 homes and nearly all of them use Bpay, If Joe Criminal pulls it off he can be in China using Chinese banking laws to protect nearly One Million Australian Dollars for a good month before anyone even knows something's wrong and if China doesn't grant Joe asylum he can simply hop across the border to a non-extradition country.

Another example of high paying cons is simply listing big ticket items for sale via eBay or associated sites and after receiving payment simply make it look as though the item was sent and got misplaced somewhere in transit this way the insurance for the item covers the loss, not you personally.

All through the late nineties and early noughties the ecommerce scene grew so quickly that this type of fraud would be really hard to prove or even identify, additionally as a precaution you would simply change your account every so often to avoid detection. These are pretty loose examples of shifty cons that also involve fraud, another pet hate, and they are probably flawed (especially in today's world) but they are still examples of how someone without any moral compass can exploit others for personal gain.

Chapter 16
The Reasons I Am Me

I think it's cliché that many people who find themselves on the wrong side of prison bars like to blame society and everyone but themselves, ultimately there's only one person in this world responsible for your actions.

While I may not have had the pleasure of a functional family and experienced more than my share of hardships as a kid, add to that the fact that I've had an undiagnosed and untreated mental disorder since who knows whilst living through stresses that I hope very few have to endure, homelessness, non-communication with one's own family for nearly eight years, rejection from certain social circles, ridicule from elitists and academics that should know better etcetera, I know that I made the conscious decision to do the things I did, things that were wrong, point blank wrong.

Though to give you a little insight into why I am/was so crazy at the time there are a couple of anecdotes I'd like to share with you. As previously mentioned I had a less than normal childhood largely due to a situation that will also help explain my natural distrust of Australian law enforcement types, my father, who shall remain nameless in this publication, was unfortunate enough to share the exact same name as a rather infamous underworld figure and although my Dad was/is a good bloke and generally a law abiding bloke to boot, he found himself working with some less than good natured people.

Dad was a very successful pro boxer until his world turned to shit one night on the way home from his second job as security on the door of one of Sydney's popular (though gangster owned) venues 'The 33 club'. One of the gangster types Dad was working with at the time was catching a ride home with Dad when they were stopped by a local Officer, unbeknown to Dad his passenger had a warrant out for his arrest and the second the cop ID'd him this guy drew a revolver and shot him in the abdomen at which point naturally Dad sped off with a slightly higher than usual heart rate.

Fortunately for all concerned the officer survived, unfortunately for Dad it was his car used in the shooting so naturally he was wanted now also and considered at large and dangerous, having never really been in any trouble before Dad naively figured he could just turn himself over for questioning and explain the whole thing. Whilst on his way to do so, in a different car driven by a friend officers gave chase again having ID'd Dad's friend as a known associate in passing. Dad's friend not wanting a bar of this pulled over and Dad quickly legged it while being shot at by some rather angry coppers, apparently they were judge, jury and executioner back in the day. With the help of some family friends Dad found his way to New Zealand and got some much-needed surgery on his nose- much needed as he had difficulty breathing because of the boxing and also as the Doc altered his nose to the extent where Dad no longer looked that much like the guy everyone was looking for. Shortly after getting to NZ Dad met Mum, I remember pictures of Dad pre and post op and having a giggle at the hippy white guy afro Dad was sporting at the time which were all the rage of the era, he probably did this purely for disguise, he told Mum that he was using an assumed identity and came clean about his predicament rather early on I believe so the two of them had no secrets. What made the situation even more fragile was that Dad's real identity (real name) as mentioned was the same as a very bad character wanted by authorities in other countries as well as NZ and OZ and this guy's last known whereabouts was actually New Zealand so it took great trust for Mumsy to give Dad a chance , so anyway at the time my folks seemed to really love each other, that's what I tell myself anyway, as one night shortly after meeting Mum and Dad were in a hotel in Christchurch and I was conceived, *'choice!'* ,so the story goes.

For as long as I can remember my family has always been very transient, by that I mean we were always on the move, I'd only just get used to living somewhere and we'd have to up and move again. Naturally this wasn't an environment conducive to good mental health, not that I'm blaming my parents I'd say it's more to do with my own idiosyncrasies than anything. It wasn't until I was about twelve years old that I even discovered the reasons behind my constant upheaval and I had to hear it from my dodgy bikie step father, my parents separated when I was 7 and

Mum married a douche bag, this guy was actually a pretty okay and cool guy however not exactly responsible parent material and this was overstated in the way he informed me of my families past. This jerk told me that my Dad was a criminal, which in effect was true in that he fled the scene of a crime, though Dad didn't bring any of the bullshit that happened on himself at will, and Step Father of the year didn't bother explaining that to me he just told me he was a criminal. As you can imagine hearing this about the guy you've looked up to all your life and depended on was pretty earth shattering. Luckily at that age I still had the maturity to give Dad the benefit of the doubt and asked Mum who quickly told me what really happened, so following the initial discussion with Step Douche our relationship quickly went downhill and I was moved back to live with Dad, win-win for me I say!

Dad had a house on the Mid-North Coast in a little country town I had spent some of my child hood and I found myself catching up with old friends and was genuinely glad to be there for a while until the awkward teenage years came and Dad not being equipped with the parenting tools of the time was more inclined to express himself through violence than dialogue, I must reaffirm the fact that I am not trying to sound like a victim here I actually was a little shit at school and didn't apply myself and if I had access to a time machine would in fact travel back to kick my 'own' arse. So any way Dad and I got a bit distant from each other after I was starting to catch up to him in terms of size and my senior year, which I completed while holding a job at a local hotel, Dad moved south to buy a business and some of my friends moved in, which in retrospect was the dumbest thing ever. Dad's house was a little three bedroom place with a study he'd converted into a fourth so when I had four other friends there relegating myself to the lounge and these guys didn't even really contribute to the rent add to which one of them had his bitchy girlfriend move in too, oh and a dog now lived in my old room too, let's not forget that, then this was a recipe for disaster.

During all this crap I somehow, just barely, passed my HSC around the time Dad left and following several nervous breakdowns which in hindsight were possibly full blown mental breakdowns. When the house situation became too much I left and moved out west then back to a major city working in many industries and usually doing quite well at them though nothing really seemed to make me want to stay, perhaps the nomadic life was now part of my repertoire.

Earlier I mentioned an attempt to join the ADF via direct entry and it was at that point I headed to Western Australia to pursue a role in the mines, so I sold all my worldly possessions on Ebay and bought a one way ticket to Perth then travelled up to Kalgoorlie where I undertook the necessary training to apply for positions underground and low and behold the second company I approached said 'Can you start Monday?'.

All was going well until the GFC hit a few years later and I happened to be on voluntary unpaid leave at the time which meant I didn't even get severances pay, this situation wasn't the worst of it though, I soon had difficulty finding a place to live and had to be less selective about where I could go which was a big mistake, when I finally did get a place after a very brief and uninformative inspection I soon discovered I was living in a predicament not un-similar to the one at my Dad's old place ie; it was a three bedroom joint that had about four-five people living in it the thing that 'was' noticeably un-similar however was the fact that my new housemates were actually ice heads, In Western Australia there is a big drug culture and a strong presence of crystal- meth amphetamine.

So with no job and stuck with these psychos while quickly running out of money I was running out of options and marbles. The noise these idiots made kept me up 24/7 and after about two weeks of no real sleep I found myself manic and full of adrenalin. We lived in a very dodgy part of town (Perth not Kal) near an old amusement park and using my sudden rush of energy and manic strength I was literally leaping over fences and running around like some sort of berserk adrenalin junkie, at one point I'd climbed on top of a replica castle constructed of fibreglass and I have no idea how what I did is even possible I mean this thing doesn't even have any holds or actual holes for foot holds or grips anywhere on the thing and I was upside down on the roof and the fucking thing is 12 metres high, then in some fantastic euphoric adventure I decide to scale the outside of the bungee platform, knowing in my gut what this would lead to, this in itself was risky as the structure is encased in a poorly welded mesh which supported my weight until I got to the top when I got there I laid there all night contemplating all manner of crazy profound concepts all the while checking the wind and realising I had no way of knowing the depth of the water below or if I could even hit it as from this height (40 metres- I googled it) it looked like a freakin puddle.

So as the sun starts to rise from the other side of Oz I'm excited and scared of the probability of survival and as I wait there backed up to the edge hoping for the wind to change and start blowing toward me a kind of calm realization, not unlike the one experienced during my arrest, washes over me and I just let myself fall backwards slowly and luckily I controlled the drop/spin fairly well though when I hit the water I must have been doing a fairly decent rate of knots as I don't think I've ever felt an impact like that and I've been in a total of nine various vehicle accidents thus far. When I finally emerged from the tannin stained water smelling like 'I don't know what' I remembered hitting the water and seeing nothing but red as if I were immersed in blood, then I clamoured out onto the grass and lay there spewing and coughing up blood.

Following that I limped away meekly and climbed over a security fence to quickly find I'd jumped into a property protected by some rather large angry canines, at this point I looked so freaky I think the mutts were more curious than angry, anyway I created a bit of a spectacle when I limped into a nearby Red Rooster dripping stinking water everywhere and with eyes as red as a zombie, the Dr would later tell me that I had burst most of the blood vessels in my eyes, torn some lung tissue and fractured my lower right leg, then I ordered a quarter chicken and chips with gravy and I have to say it was the most amazing thing I've ever eaten! I suspect this was purely out of my gratitude at my second chance. Given what I had just done, I honestly wasn't sure if I would survive at the time, and it would have been easy for me to knock myself unconscious and drown. Luckily for me some good Samaritans saw that I needed help and drove me to hospital.

The above is one factual account from my past that is totally off the scale freakin nuts, but what is crazier still is I often think about what happened that day, even right now as I write this, and think wow what a rush that was and I'm kind of, I won't say glad, but 'excited' that it happened and that I'm still alive.

While there are surely those that will dismiss the above as lies, I can assure you it happened and for curiosities sake you may like to use a search engine to look up the world's highest tower dive- you will find that decades ago some looney Yank in speedos did a triple reversal backflip off a 156ft or 52Metre tower and did it flawlessly and the whole thing's on Youtube. I might add that his jump makes what I did look like a total anti-climax.

Chapter 17
Having Your Hands Tied

Somewhere amidst the writing of this book I found myself working as a carpenter for a business under my ABN following a meeting with two of the directors. It was a shonky operation from the beginning and I was well aware of the fact that these guys were using what are known as sham contracts- Employing/exploiting contractors that are technically employees by paying them a very low rate without any of the mandatory benefits ie: superannuation, tax, sick pay and other entitlements while earning a tonne of money charging them out as qualified/licensed contractors etcetera.

This fact however was not the problem, I was totally prepared to cop the low rate as I was doing so many hours that I was still doing quite well anyway and getting great experience at the same time. What was a real issue unfortunately was the fact that these idiots (the directors, not anyone else there) were adding insult to injury by treating the guys and I like snot and paying us late, not paying for travel despite up to 100 minutes travel each way some days and then the final straw, following a late payment 'yet again' despite an early invoice and a very diplomatic request for timely payment I asked for a payment confirmation via

SMS. Well given the verbal assault I received from the 5ft pencil pushing director, who didn't know the first thing about actual work, you'd think I asked for his daughter's virginity!

So an hour or two passed when I got another call and here I am thinking he'd calmed down and called to apologise, fuck me! This halfwit unloaded on me again to the point where I had to tell him how it was, low and behold his dickhead partner jumps on the phone and starts trying to sound all heavy thinking it'd scare me, totally oblivious to the fact that I'm starting to get so pissed off I'm on my way to the car thinking *'Fuck parole! This cunt's dead!'* and I'm in the car keeping this poser on the line engine running telling him to be there at the showroom when 'all of a sudden' he's not going to be there all afternoon! This is after he's had the gall to call me a 'little cunt' etc.

I was that pissed off that I still wanted this cunt dead hours later when he said he would be there, which is precisely when I was on my way there to return the poofy shirts these wankers had us wearing.

To paint a picture (without prejudging based on race) this guy was a Lebanese bloke with zero trade experience and a second generation rich bitch who was basically given a business, no trade background and no fucking idea, he was a big guy but without exaggeration I've seriously fucked up bigger and tougher blokes. So I was looking forward to beating the shit out of him when I arrived at the showroom, adrenalin pumping and half expecting a few of his cousins to be there as enforcers.

In retrospect I was lucky this guy was a total pussy and "just happened" to have the longest meeting in history that day and subsequently never came to the showroom. I'm positive I would have annihilated him and following his threats would've wanted to make a point of giving him something to remember, broken arm, nose, jaw etc. Though I only had the intention of letting these urges get the better of me on the day as after I calmed down the obvious danger of spending a long time in a bad, bad place became very real again and I think the fact that I couldn't turn up on any given day and belt this prick probably pissed me off even more. It's funny but even as a law abiding citizen it would have been as simple as making one or two anonymous phone calls on these dickheads, one to fair work informing them of the sham operations and a second to the Australian taxation office alerting them to the obvious tax evasion these idiots were committing, however this would have gone against my somewhat stubborn code of ethics and inmates and cons would have considered it a 'dog act' which it kind of would have been. So to this day I haven't done anything despite the fact that this wanker had me so angry I was literally out for blood, even writing this and recounting the events and conversations of that day I find my blood boiling so it's probably for the best that I don't actively go anywhere near this dickhead as I think I'd loose control and have to hurt him… a lot.

Not long after I left having stayed in touch with a few of the other guys I found that they were wise to the bullshit there too and had taken it a few steps further. It seemed karma was catching up to these pricks, the last I had heard they were struggling to keep any employees and had lost a lot of really big contracts, if things kept up this way they would be entering administration.

As it turns out it was a huge silver lining to end my dealings with these idiots anyway as I applied for a similar role immediately and found myself not only getting paid on time, but being paid what I was worth, well almost. Not too long after that role I would be offered a position with a small family operation that paid extremely well and was just a short commute from my Unit, which I eventually left briefly to an offer at the local Council as a safety officer which appealed to me as being a government employee has its security and perks however when I eventually got tired of being so underworked and overlooked for promotion, I was promoted once by the way, after two years I went back to the family operation where there is a high level of morale and a great culture, when I think back to the crazy idiotic Arabs that sent me into a rage I am amazed and annoyed with myself that I didn't apply for a better role right away.

Take it from me that if you ever find yourself hating your job or even simply wishing for more don't be afraid to put it out there and just apply, you never know how things could improve.

One thing I did manage to do while I was at the Council was in my own time I enrolled in a Business Diploma and as I have a vested interest in business found it extremely interesting which is probably why I cruised through the course, completing and passing the Diploma a full nine months ahead of the set time, I enjoyed it so much that I have looked at more courses and am due to enrol again soon, perhaps even matriculating into something like an MBA one day.

While all of this has vastly improved my employability, I am for the moment quite happy right where I am as my bosses, my co-workers and my team are great, I look forward to getting up in the morning and spending the next eight-ten hours laughing and smiling while just getting things done.

So if I could impress one thing upon the younger people out there that maybe didn't have the best start at school and perhaps are stuck in a role you hate, or have no role at all, think about something you might be passionate about, or even just interested in and enrol in some course of study and if you can focus on your strengths, if you are good with numbers choose something associated with accounting etc, if you are a great communicator select something in this area, you have nothing to loose and everything to gain.

Chapter 18
Ranting

I think somewhere along the way I told myself I was going to avoid ranting, preaching and attempting to impose my views on readers, at the end of the day your views are simply that.

Though you may recall in the blurb of this book it states an intention to impart some insight on the folly of offenders! It kind of goes both ways as the world isn't black and white, as much as some of us would like it to be.

At the time of writing, again, there has been controversy surrounding another fatal shooting by police and despite my best intentions to seem impartial on this subject I'd just like to say you'd have to be too stupid to be literate if you take offence to my remarks here.

Any idiot can see that when a junkie, mental patient or even an actual violent criminal has a knife it would be relatively easy to simply disable that person or incapacitate them with standard issue Tasers, their intended purpose, rather than having several trigger happy monkeys with guns and badges lethally unload more rounds than necessary on the 'Victim's' centre mass.

I intentionally use this word (victim) as when a person armed with a 10cm knife has as many as 5 shots, this information is reliant on witnesses testimony as the Police have closed ranks and hindered reports, unloaded in their chest when the same monkeys have spray, tasers and a freakin K9 response unit at their disposal that is precisely what they are 'Victims'.

Not too many people seemed to have factored that little chestnut into their equations- It was a dog squad unit that shot this bloke! Hello?, fuck me, why even have the dogs if not to subdue some nutter with a knife, yes I know they are used for tracking, rescue, drug detection, bomb detection and a lot more.

Before some 'I only see black and white' know all scalds me for suggesting that the dogs don't deserve to be in harm's way I can tell you this, this isn't the movies if one or more pissed off, trained police dogs sees you with a knife or even senses you are a threat when they're simply let off their chain, you won't be harming anyone or holding onto the knife for long!

And just in case you missed the point every single time you've witnessed any footage of police dogtraining- That's what they're trained for!

Unless you've been living as a hermit your entire adult life or are such a recluse that you haven't really had any real social contact you would/should be aware that there are those among us that are idealistic and like to approach problems in a rational and logical way also there are many levels of personality within the human spectrum and conversely there are those that seek out authority based on some narcissistic urge to belittle and repress, for example 'some' police officers, 'most' parole officers and almost 'all' politicians I think are a pretty good example of the negative. I think even the best intentioned and pure police officer couldn't deny that they feel a certain thrill using the power of the badge and like most logical people I find it irritating when seemingly average people are so oblivious to this problem.

Following the above mentioned shooting which was unfortunately one of many, somehow and seemingly unapologetically scores of people took to social media to express their views on the matter, showing no consideration for the deceased's family and often spouting all manner of brown nosing support for the killers, AKA- the police, even making such outrageous statements like "He got what was coming".

The man suffered with a history of mental illness for god's sake and while that doesn't give him the right to threaten, a little shiny metal thing with the word police printed on it damn sure doesn't give you the right to use him as close quarters target practice!

Here's a social experiment for you- I propose we create a hypothesis for children and in it we outline all of the facts in the above scenario though don't bring 'the law' into it or the location just the stats and dress it up as a fictitious project for say- years two-three as your average seven to eight year old, eight to nine if you're slow, will be able to show you just how fucking dumb, backwards and pro-cop stubborn most adults have become. I'm not going to preach to you that I have all the answers and that I'm not biased or infallible, but if you think for a second that an unbiased, impartial child would approve of killing a man with a history of mental illness with more than one officer firing lethally on him, failing to use their spray and their tasers and most importantly their dogs, for which they are trained then I think you are more than a little confused.

If you haven't thrown the book down in disgust and issued a death warrant on me, you may also like to know I don't envy the officers in the situation mentioned and that I am aware their job isn't easy.

Though one thing I find incredibly odd when I hear these sorts of arguments (I say 'hear' as I seldom participate for fear of murdering someone) is often the same idiots that apparently think a badge literally means a cop can bend you over and rape you without question are so supportive of murderous officers yet well vehemently condemn the shit out of any "wrong doing" by a serving member of an allied force ie – touching the remains of an enemy combatant, even if it's just to check for booby traps. Oh fuck and heaven forbid these people that live under 'actual threat' every day and night of deployment fire first as it's against ROE!

Gee I wonder if the same twat monkeys who spout so

much "I support Officers" BS would be happy to jump on twitter or Facebook telling everyone that a jihadist 'got what was coming' if the guy was armed only with a fucking knife!

Not fucking likely! Please understand that my use of profanity is to A; help punctuate the message and B; make a fucking point!

In real life I hardly swear, honestly most people scarcely believe I've been in trouble!

In any case I hope that for those that may have been on the fence or disinterested in the problems of Australian Law enforcement have at the very least tried to consider the situation from the perspective of others. Also if you are offended and still reading then you may like to know that when you put all your bull shit in writing supporting police and others abusing positions of trust and power there's no little points system, just like people who drive around with 'cops are tops' stickers on. If you're speeding chances are you will still receive a ticket, the officer might take advantage of the free BJ your sticker entitles him to, but that's about it.

Chapter 19
Dumb-Shit

I think it's safe to say that the average person wouldn't expect to hear too many words of wisdom or seek enlightenment in a prison. Surprisingly however it's not all that unusual to meet brighter than average guys that are wasting away their talents, of course there's always an abundance of total and utter stupidity on tap in any correctional centre too, so after witnessing a great deal of this idiocy first hand I thought I had better jot some of it down as a lot of it is just too funny. Here I'll explain quotes and actual events, most of which took place in the "special needs unit" aka the psycho ward.

In the realm of the criminally insane there are about five or six guys that made a long-lasting impression on my life, two of them I suspect may have actually been father and son and not have even known it. As usual for the purpose of the book we'll just refer to them as Gary and Scott, Gary was a sloth of a man that appeared at first glance to be as old as you can get before dropping. If I saw him in a retirement home and was unaware of his lifestyle choices, I'd assume he was one hundred plus years old, that is of course until he spoke, which was often, or did anything physical which was constantly.

Scott looked almost identical in facial features and had the same spectre like speed abuse discolouration that speed freaks eventually get in their irises and he was of similar gait and posture though a full head taller and carried a bit more muscle, as mentioned earlier when a patient/prisoner gets manic, ie restless and/or agitated, they often display symptoms like unnatural strength and endurance and Gary had these qualities in spades. Scott too had these traits and I suspect that sleeping was of little importance to either of them. So here I am in the nutter unit doing my best not to attract attention from officers or convicts when eventually both these monkeys wound up in the unit and it wasn't long before they were at each other's throats. One incident in particular that stands out happened the day after a long and colourful display of profanity and abusive language followed by some brief fisty cuffs and a swift march to the acting warden's office. The morning started with the kind of tense anticipation you'd expect when there was one too many alpha nuts in the nut house. Initially I was impressed as Scott, the biggest psycho of them all, to his credit seemed to be un-phased by the events of the previous day and for most part just went about his usual routine unbelievably oblivious to Gary's taunts. This continued for a full ten minutes until almost all of the unit was watching expectantly, even I was taking note, usually I avoided spectacles as they almost always ended in bloodshed and more grief.

So here's Scott calmly leaning against a wall much, much quieter than usual the whole time some nutty ancient sloth of a spectre like man hurling all manner of abuse at him when all of a sudden cool as a cucumber Scott moves in a smooth action and scoops Gary up in an elbow through the crotch wrestler hold and dumps him head first into the nearest otto bin! You could hear the immediate protesting blurt out of this old fruits mouth even when he was upside down covered in all manner of horrible crap, legs kicking away in a fit of anger so intense that he almost got out if it himself. In the end the officers were so busy trying not to laugh that they took a good while to help the old bastard out of the thing.

Unfortunately for me Scott suffered from paranoid psychosis, among other things, and started telling guys in the special needs unit that I was an undercover cop, *For fuck's sake! This isn't the fucking departed.* And due to the level of stupidity in this place this story actually gained more momentum than you would expect, when I started confronting guys that were acting shadier than usual they'd mutter what they'd heard and then say things like 'I dunno what to believe mate, I just don't wanna get involved'. In other words they knew it was bullshit but they were too gutless to oppose it. Eventually I found out it was him and as any con will tell you there is only one way to deal with this, so naturally we ended up fighting, fortunately for Scott I am not a heartless killer as I hope readers have surmised by now as had he pulled this crap on any of the lifers he would have almost certainly been shanked and then some. Shortly after this incident I was sentenced and transferred out of remand to an actual Prison as opposed to a remand centre, this in itself is a whole other story which I will attend to soon.

One guy I met, we'll call him Ed, was a nice enough bloke, very knowledgeable and academic enough to have qualified for and fulfilled a master's degree under an indigenous scholarship. When I found myself needing advice regarding the university admissions testing that I was completing it was Ed that I would turn to for answers, that is of course until I realised he was a bit of a nutter, this was bound to be the case though after all poor old Ed had been incarcerated since before I had finished high school, eventually though it all became a bit much. One day Ed was telling a group of us students how humans were descended from certain animals, it wasn't Darwinian theory Ed was preaching though he had specifically said while most white men had evolved from apes his particular tribe were all descended, not from a humanoid biped like an ape, but from crows, that's right, from a bird. I didn't want to touch this subject with a twenty foot didgeridoo so I just sort of quietly slunk away in the retarded Q & A that followed, all the while wondering if Ed had considered what the links in between this evo/devolution would look like and or why there was no fossil evidence of such a crazy claim, not to mention the implications that the whole 'Ed you are only 1/8th indigenous' conversation would create. I do realise that when a person identifies as an aboriginal they are accepted one hundred percent as an indigenous Australian, much in the way that my brother, from a different father, is simply my brother not my half brother. This does not somehow change the genetic material within ones DNA however, for example if eighty seven point five percent of

Ed's genetic material actually comes from the same part of the gene pool as mine then in his crazy birdman theory even he has to concede that very little of his DNA can be traced to the bush turkey or what ever.

This next anecdote is reliant on the account of a third party as I wasn't there to witness it, luckily for me. My mate Johnny who was in and out all his life, mostly for assaulting those that would assault him, had a story from his early days that when I think of it makes me chuckle at times. Johnny starting early found himself at the notorious Boggah road Prison way back when he had only just become an adult and could be tried as one. Being a young bloke and chucked in at the deep end in Boggah road would have been daunting enough without having to fight off hardened crazies or living under threat of sexual assault.

Though it seemed that one of the inmates had taken a liking to Johnny and was openly threatening young Johnny with rape, often exposing himself to Johnny and telling him to perform all manner of sexual acts, this would take place in full view of other inmates and the corrections staff often without any intervention from either party.

One day Johnny had had enough and not being easily intimidated he had devised a plan of sorts, after breakfast when this thug usually started up Johnny was mentally prepared for what would follow and for what this nutter was unlikely to expect and when he started making his way toward Johnny, who'd strategically positioned himself near the yard door, that's when it happened.

Johnny was sitting with his back against the yard wall by the door as if he were a stereo typical Mexican in a western taking a siesta, and when the creepy inmate approached with himself exposed as usual Johnny did something unexpected saying 'What do you want me to do with that?' to which the inmate replied 'give me a BJ' Johnny says 'well give it here then'. The nut job actually believing that Johnny was about to give him oral gratification stupidly wanders close enough for Johnny to grab him by the sack with his left and unleash a flurry of devastating crosses with his right, over and over in quick succession, having had a pre beat down chat with some of the other inmates, also fed up with this thug, two of them had quickly closed the yard door and now lent against it hard, stopping any intervention by the screws until they saw fit. Apparently, Mr rapist began squealing like a stuck pig and not being short of strength or speed Johnny had done quite a bit of damage before he'd finally decided this scum had had enough, this wasn't before Mr scumbag had started to loose consciousness mind you. This my friends is a classic story of prison yard justice and I'm told that the medical staff and screws were reluctant to administer much in the way of treatment as this goon had created more than a few casualties in the past. In any case young Johnny was instantly a popular guy and commanded much more respect amongst his peers, I think Johnny tells the story better and if you knew him you'd know why, despite the fact that poor old Johnny is a jail head and had a rough trot, he has got to be hands down one of the most charismatic and funny people I've ever had the pleasure of knowing, seldom a dull moment when Johnny's about.

While in the special needs unit another incident, also involving Scott and Gary, I witnessed was almost a very unpleasant experience for all, not long after the Gary garbage stuffing incident Scott had gotten even angrier and through what must have been sheer manic strength literally picked up a petrol- powered gurney, lid opened, and doused old Gaz with the petrol from it promptly took a long draw on a cigarette and flicked it at him.

Fortunately, it failed to ignite and we didn't have to witness the horror of seeing an old man burned alive in the yard, I was fairly certain as Scott's 'burn the old man to death' plan unfolded that this would happen and I wasn't too worried, I was more amazed at the strength this nutcase displayed when he raised a forty- fifty odd kilo irregular shaped gurney over his head and just had to laugh at the lunacy of it all.

Chapter 20
The Far East

At the time of writing this I'm somewhere between nursing myself back from suicidal tendencies and trying to get this thing published, having finally submitted a manuscript to a publisher, thanks guys by the way!

Stuck in that region in eastern Oz that is known for its tourism after the disaster that was my new life with a certain Barbie doll like eastern European, I don't have much to keep myself occupied other than to write and attempt to vent some of my frustrations. If it wasn't for the fact that one of my most caring and loyal friends lives here and has graciously offered me temporary accommodation following my split with what's her face, I think I would have had a full blown melt down and perhaps crossed a few lines where her male "friends" health and safety is concerned because I am just beyond caring at this point.

I actually have the opportunity to head back to my old work as my boss is an absolute legend and adamant that there will always be a job for me, though I just don't want to give up on this place, also my Mum's residence is not too far from here and she isn't in the best of health. In any case as seems the norm my local parole officer is rather slow and under the impression that I'm the one who needs things explained to 'me' with care. Upon meeting her the first time several red flags immediately went up, as she'd scheduled the meeting for ten a.m. which I had triple checked with her on the phone while it was on speaker, at this point I was still with what's her face, and she was in agreement with me that it was ten a.m. and not later. So I'm sitting there until eleven five when the new officer finally turns up without offering an explanation and certainly nothing in the way of an apology and then tells me she'd made the appointment for ten thirty which would have meant she was still thirty five minutes late irrespective. As you can imagine it was difficult to be in good spirits by this stage, even before this person had waddled all of her 130+ kgs through the door it was obvious that like many government employees she was taking advantage of some kind of affirmative action role (I'm not making reference to her gender) in that she was obviously eligible for disability, both physically and otherwise. So, any way I spent the rest of the meeting winning her over and honestly explaining that I never intend to break any laws again etcetera, and finally we part ways with me thinking we are on the same page. Little did I know this woman was dafter than I'd given credit, it turns out that without my consent or any reason rather than confirm my address with me via invoices, she'd actually called the caravan park that we'd checked into and made them aware of my status, I couldn't believe it! I promptly called the office for an explanation and this twit became verbally hostile when I asked her if that was how she handled things would she be likely to try this with my employers, next thing I know she's trying to tell me I'm legally required to inform not only my employers but anyone I have significant contact with. Thankfully my old Officer back in a certain city is not only really switched on and a nice guy, but was prepared to defend me against this idiot and her boss who as it turned out tried to claim the same BS as her. The scary thing about this shit is I'm sure many guys that get out are unaware of their rights and just cop this crap, there's no telling just how many reasonable or at least qualified guys have missed out on work thanks to fuckwads like this, and this is supposed to aid society 'how' exactly?

So after winning this idiot over 'again' I spent the next few visits attempting to build a repour with her and mentioned at length the hurdles I have had to overcome intentionally trying to make her aware of the fact that not only was her bullshit counterproductive but most likely to result in one of her offenders reoffending, in addition I actually tried to use her for her intended purpose and gain some actual guidance and insight into how to go about volunteering and applying myself for the community, which I am actually sincere about in that ultimately I'd like to help with the Careflight lifesaver operation and have done much research into how to go about being involved and whether or not a criminal check is likely to preclude any service from yours truly.

As it turns out following all I could find on the net you can in fact volunteer as a lifesaver upon successful completion of the bronze medallion and Careflight generally recruit from the lifesavers, to ad to my prospects I would undergo further training at my own expense in the form of loadmaster certification and whichever paramedical training I can fulfil given my past transgressions. Now I'm not sure if Parole officer of the year just assumed I was full of it or whether she was just particularly nasty but at my next appointment which was only a week after the last, she made me wait again and then had me see her boss, Oh my God! This woman truly is gifted in the department of stupidity, having spoken to her on the phone I had tried to prepare myself for some painfully slow conversation but fuck me! Yet again this cretin was totally convinced that she had to treat 'me' like a child and not the other way around. Upon entering her interview room I became aware that in her mind I was on some sort of trial and that I should treat her with some kind of reverence, she was concerned when I didn't jump through hoops and act like I was the nicest guy in the world, this became obvious when after answering the exact same question (How are you today) for the third time with the exact same response (fine) she, in her ever monotone and painfully slow voice, said 'I'm going to assume that you're not well today Mitchell'. I simply told her with as much disinterest as I could muster 'I'm just here to attend an appointment, that's all'. She then went through the painfully long and overly thorough list of my parole conditions as if this was her little 'making a difference' contribution for the day, at any point when I queried her on a subject listed in my conditions, which she often didn't have any real understanding of, she would just repeat 'This is part of your conditions, and you are lawfully required to comply' rather than actually answer any of my questions for which she wasn't really equipped any way. By the end of the appointment I'd had about all I could handle of her smug expression and mindless dribble, I'm sure my body language made it obvious that I was less than impressed with this persons opinion of how I was supposed to be treated, but eventually I just had to concede that I had to deal with this bullshit.

As I've mentioned before, normally I refrain from bad language and make a point of being well mannered so when I finally cracked and used the words 'bullshit' she was caught by surprise, so then I followed it up with 'This is Fucking bullshit'. This is usually a bad way to go as although these people can't just breach you for bad language failure to participate in their little games often means they'll just invent some reason for you to be breached any way. I then went on to explain that I wasn't going to play her little game and that I didn't have to pretend to like her, then I told her point blank that I don't like her and I hope that she gets a thrill out of her little job. I admit that what I said sounds a bit juvenile, but there's only so much you can say to these idiots and I literally had to put it in the most basic English possible to avoid confusion. Following this crap, I attempted to contact my PO three times that afternoon in an effort to reschedule my next appointment as they'd deliberately set it right in the middle of business hours. If you've ever had the displeasure of dealing with a parole order you are most likely painfully aware that it is virtually impossible to get hold of most of them before ten a.m. and they're usually finished by two-thirty three p.m., often do very little and make a tidy sum at the tax payer's expense, it was this sort of utter shit that had Parole Officer of the year trying to make me visit right in the middle of business hours as if her time, or at least the finite amount she actually spent at work, was more important than 'my' work time.

So finally on the following Monday I get hold of her and despite being as neutral and diplomatic about the cluster fuck that was last week, she still ends up talking to me as if I'm four years old and then gets abusive when I start giving it back to her eventually hanging up, dog.

As previously mentioned in Australia due to the Privacy Act former convicts are entitled to refrain from disclosing their criminal pasts unless they are convicted of SVOs, serious violent offences, sexual assault, or fraud. If you are Australian and you are not aware of this then you may want to do a lot more reading, if you are from North America and disagree with this I would suggest that the number of serial reoffenders would drop dramatically and rehabilitation would actually have a chance if this Act was adopted by your country, though I do believe that minor offences in some states aren't required to be reported to employers your loose privacy laws mean that anyone can perform a background check, thankfully here the only ones with the power are government agencies and law enforcement, as it should be.

Chapter 21
Transfers

Earlier you will recall I mentioned that an individual can be held without charge for up to three years. For myself due to the high profile of the case it wasn't that long, which was both good and bad, good in that I would at least be given what's know as a top and bottom. Top, being the maximum duration of my stay at Rancho Relaxo, and bottom being my earliest date of eligibility for parole. I had actually served over a year in custody before my day in court and for this fiasco of a hearing I would once again rendezvous with Pol-Air and get flung back to the town-city of my offences to face my "peers".

My old man had brought my suit along for me on my last visit for this reason and I'd spent all I had on a pair of prison issue glasses in my prescription in an effort to make me look less menacing, unbeknown to me I would have my glasses held outside the courtroom as at that stage my classification was high and I was deemed a flight risk, *Mmmmm yeah cause I was totally going to pick my handcuffs and slay the several officers in court needed to make my escape using a cheap pair of Dior knockoffs.*

So there I am sweating like a Pedo in a sandpit having

had to wear dark jeans with my suit jacket given that my recent potato rich Prison diet in combination with extremely limited exercise had me too fat to wear the suit pants on this occasion. Doing my best to look like that of a confused and misguided recently diagnosed mental patient who doesn't present any real threat to anyone, which I'll be honest actually was the case. My Dad had come along for moral support and to at least show the Court that I had a small network of support upon my release.

Of all the emotions that I experienced that day the most profound was shame, a deep sense of shame. Myself, BA and the "victims" knew what had actually happened and this didn't make it any easier, simply being involved in this whole idiotic idea in any way was simply inexcusable. Despite the fact that BA and I made it overly non-threatening, giving just the right amount of *'I'm so desperate I might be dangerous despite my impeccable manners'* The "victims" had written impact statements. Anyone with half a brain would be aware that these people would be entitled to a tidy sum in the form of compensation and the more they played up their "suffering" the more they were likely to pocket. This coupled with the fact that they would've been rightly pissed off with myself and BA meant that almost all of them just went to town with their stories, not so much in their recollection of the events but more in terms of their coping afterwards. I'm not so blind as to pretend that even with the level of care we showed it had to still be somewhat confronting having two black clad loonies surprise you at night and take something that wasn't theirs. But what these people spouted sounded a lot like something

Lionel Hutz (of The Simpsons) would have you rehearse. Following their damning statements and the fact we were pleading guilty I think the Judge would have been inclined to throw the book at us, save for a few small details, one being my untreated illness and two being the huge strides BA had made in terms of good behaviour and his very genuine letters he read aloud in court apologising profusely and honestly in the most eloquent fashion I think I've ever witnessed firsthand, he is quite the writer.

As it turned out my sentence would carry a top of six years and a bottom of two, which meant that following the year plus I'd already served I would be eligible for parole in around another twelve months and the rest of my sentence would be fore filled in a maximum security setup which actually had a residential section, before anyone gets delusions of town houses and/or apartment blocks I will tell you that the resi section is still extremely depressing and can be even more dangerous than general population because if anything ever goes down in your block you need to be able to survive for quite a while before any would be help ever turns up. Irrespective of the relative tranquillity of residential I had to apply, pass and be wait-listed like everyone else trying to get out of hell, when I use the term hell I don't think I'm exaggerating as much as it may sound, the layout in the older part of this prison seemed to help the final remaining part of one's imagination die. Cold stale and sterile looking walls with ultrahigh ceilings offering small and scarce windows every once-in a while to let in whatever little natural light is available at the time creating an overall medieval theme to this dark and demonic looking misery hole. Even though we were in the tropics it seemed to have rained even more than it should have back when I was awaiting resi status. Eventually it came and not a moment too soon it seems because I had found myself in one of the more dodgy units of the prison and one of few white guys to boot. Once in res I started working at the kitchen while I awaited the opportunity to study and pass the University admissions exam, which I did, all the while avoiding trouble and presenting as a reformed criminal awaiting parole.

Finally, the opportunity to apply for parole came up and I had actually written, re written and rehearsed exactly what I would and would not say at the hearing. With spiels and retorts and everything, it was a dicey panel in that it consisted entirely of woman all too eager to cut a man off at the knees, fortunately for me I had still somehow managed to win them over, it wasn't easy mind you and I almost lost them to their own stupidity. When queried as to why I would use violence against others, knowing that they intended to deliberately bate me into an argument with the misuse of the term, I carefully and respectfully articulated why 'by definition' I hadn't actually used violence and why no one involved was ever in danger. At this point one of the women in particular launched into a tirade through clenched teeth in an unusually over the top display of anger, even for a DCS woman. Stating that the use of the threat of violence whether actually verbalised or just implied as it were was violent in itself and that I was lacking remorse by not acknowledging the "victims" to this I replied that I was never suggesting that they weren't victims and that I was ever remorseful of my actions and genuinely did regret ever going to these lengths and that I was simply trying to articulate the fact that no actual physical violence was used nor were the staff in any danger and that they had not been verbally threatened either. Luckily for me one of the more reasonable staff at the hearing realised that I was being completely honest and that nothing in the police report suggested otherwise and reluctantly 'miss tear my balls off' calmed down enough to agree a little and move onto the next point, a week later I got word that I was successful (successful is a relative term in that you are never really free when you are on parole).

Here at this particular prison, there was a culture of beatings and vicious attacks, one thing that I often marvel at is the ability of seemingly dull-witted individuals to suddenly become very creative when it comes to using various household items ie furniture, doors, even clothing as weapons and as I would learn there was volume upon volume of attack related story here at this place. Again, I kept a low profile and for the most part avoided any trouble though when I hit the home stretch of my sentence it was as if management was trying to make things impossible when a certain ego freak of narcissistic crim turned up in our block/unit.

This person definitely had a screw loose, I am hesitant to mention that he was part indigenous as I don't want to come across as racist though usually I'd just leave that fact out I think it's worth mentioning in that the little chip on some, not all, part aboriginal Aussies shoulders was more like a fucking mountain with this guy, he hated everyone and was prone to all manner of violent outbursts which were often indiscriminate meaning he would attack anyone, indigenous and Caucasian alike. I couldn't tell you whether or not this guy was using the knowledge of my impending release as a shield, knowing that he could get away with more shit than usual or if he genuinely welcomed the idea of having a scrap with me, either way he was a fucking nut and there were quite a few close calls, nothing that had me so pissed I'd risk throwing it all away luckily.

The guy had been inside several times all for the same reason, armed robbery, and unlike yours truly this guy actually used real guns and real ammo and although he hadn't killed anyone, at least not that we are aware of, he had fired upon civilians and used violence in his robberies which meant his classification was SVO, as eluded to previously one of the problems with this scenario is the likelihood of re offending as the inmate has to make it known to employers, co-workers and landlords that he has a serious record.

Basically, the best he could hope for is a decent break in the employment department and to just keep out of trouble, however most of these guys become total jail heads and get institutionalised in a revolving door prison life.

Anyway, when I was finally being released, I made a point of shaking his hand looking him in the eye and wishing him all the best. The last I heard he was actually doing well which I honestly hope continues because personal gripes aside if I wish bad upon my enemies it also affects others and perpetuates the problem.

At the risk of infuriating any more readers I will concede that there are a couple of tennis courts at this venue, though I never got to use them as I just stuck to my formula, avoiding people.

Chapter 22
Family and Criminal Psychology

I know that I made mention of this earlier, but I cannot stress enough how grateful I am for the support I received from my family during my incarceration and particularly following my release. Without their help I would have been virtually homeless upon parole and following the initial syndrome of being institutionalised it would have made it next to impossible to get going again. It must be so easy for guys and girls to fall into the trap of reoffending, especially if they have any skill in their chosen field be it drug trafficking, car theft or fraud and especially if their parole officer is a morbidly obese militant feminist that makes a point of trying to belittle and undermine every attempt you make to start a career.

If anything, my cockup brought us all closer together as I hadn't had any contact with my sister for eight years preceding my offence and very little from Mum and Dad too. So eventually when I decided to transfer between states/territories It was great to once again receive some much needed help from my old man in the form of temporary accommodation, in fact Dad went as far as to endure the mandatory bullshit inspections this particular part of Australia demands in spite of the fact that I had moved out months earlier with my then girlfriend, you see the reasoning behind the failure to report this fact was simple, the dwelling in question was above the landlord's house and I think that with that little chestnut of information it would be required that the lessor, or landlord be informed of my past, and even if it somehow wasn't a requirement eventually during one of the bullshit inspections, which some less than bright officers like to actually display their DCS badges as if they're cops or something, my landlord would no doubt have had a few questions.

Whether you're a staunch anti-crime only see black and white fanatic or a realist you don't have to be a genius to know that if your officer is scheduled for an inspection, and they are scheduled visits, it's probably a good idea to hide your latest batch of Meth and/or any corpses you may have on hand, basically this is just a ridiculous way of giving someone with an already over inflated sense of purpose even more of an ego boost at the taxpayer's expense.

Here is a sincere take on what could be a concise and efficient way of rehabilitating offenders, very simply just by providing parolees with a point of contact that genuinely wants to help them, keeping in mind that by helping them you may and in fact will help others indirectly, even save others, and not having some man-hating bureaucrat hell bent on living daily dramas due to some sad programming courtesy of lame Australian television or the need to compensate for failing to apply for a more prestigious branch of the government, say a council road crew, you automatically make the likelihood of rehabilitation one hundred percent more likely.

When I was in the city, I had the pleasure of dealing with one of the most down to earth guys you could hope to be your PO, the same guy that defended me against the Nazi PO that tried to inform my employers about me. His kindness in no way undermined the seriousness of the situation and he was totally thorough but fair, before he really got to know me he had given me the benefit of the doubt but was quite firm, when he realised that I was genuine about being rehabilitated and moving forward he was just a pleasure to deal with and I could see that he not only took genuine pride in his work but he was a little idealistic in that he genuinely wanted a happy ending and better life for me, it's a shame that more POs aren't like him.

During my time with this PO I did move twice and into living situations with friends, friends who had already been briefed on my "situation" and when he, my PO, had to attend the mandatory pre- inspection he was polite concise and so brief that you would have hardly noticed what had just happened if you were a fly on the wall, and as he was such a top officer, he only attended the one inspection at each residence as let's face it, any more would be a waste of everyone's time.

I mean honestly this guy really did make a difference and he didn't have to abuse a badge or shoot Anyone, all he had to do was listen and provide some minor resources in the form of phone numbers and support.

It was directly due to dealings with officers like him that made my assimilation back into society work, I mean if I only dealt with idiots, I would have made it work anyway through sheer determination but I would have had many more a rough patch and unemployment due to the stupidity and arrogance of other officers. Forgive me if I am repeating myself but the flow on effect of the negativity from some of these dodgier POs could indirectly contribute to violent crime as the whole idea is to rehabilitate convicts not manipulate and piss them off constantly, it's as if they feel they haven't done their jobs if they aren't depriving them of even more liberty.

A phrase that came up early on in my writing when inmates are incarcerated is 'We are here as punishment, not to be punished' which simply means that while we are in custody we are forfeiting our lives, family, love, work and basically everything that makes life worthwhile so there's no need to make life harder or more painful for prisoners, now if you are reading this and thinking *'Fuck prisoners, make their lives hell'*

Have you ever stopped and wondered why you feel this way? By now you should be very aware that not all prisoners are the same and that some don't even belong there, it never ceases to amaze me how many so called straight-laced normal people think that people are sent to prison to be sodomised and that they deserve it. I can confirm that there are some really horrible people in the prisons I've had the displeasure of serving in and I'm sure this is the case the world over but even in my darkest hour I would never condone the rape of anyone and fortunately for me there were no communal showers at these fine establishments, which by the way has got to be the most twisted idea ever.

In addition to trying to impart a crime free mind set on would-be criminals I'd also like to say that it goes both ways, the broader community has to stop thinking of all criminals as some larger criminals future sex toy, and while it would be fantastic to have a police force of idealists that exist to serve, the sad truth is that it's not always that way, in fact in my experience it hardly ever is.

During COVID the local laws had changed to allow folks to be mask free during 'light exercise', including walks etc. Apparently this fact was lost on one officer that I immediately disliked as I was walking with someone very dear to me and this little guy, five-ft eight" began yelling and carrying on at us for not wearing masks, funnily enough we were in the process of donning said masks as we were about to enter an ice-cream shop and this little bitch of a man kept advancing with the body language of a guy with true little-man syndrome screaming 'Wanna get smart I can still charge ya, wanna get charged do ya' meanwhile his fellow officers were all walking around the area with ridiculous swagger like they were heroes of the wild west or something. I simply cannot describe how ridiculously angry this situation made me and frightened at the same time as I had been crime free for over a decade and it could have all unravelled and put my companion in harm's way, this guy was obviously trying to get a reaction from me and potentially cause an incident. People like this little bitch should never be issued with a badge, far less a gun!

In any event, we walked away and I eventually got over it, this may seem like a so what moment for most people but I wanted to destroy that little creep with every fibre of my being, all I would need to do is et my hand on his little throat and squeeze, and when I relive that situation I find myself asking *'If my significant other wasn't there what would I have done? What would have happened?'*

Chapter 23
The Final Chapter

After spending the first half of my life as an idiot, and enjoying it, I then had the life changing experiences noted in this book and written here you have been privy to my journey through purgatory and eventually back out of the beast and into society. However, I have discovered that my patience and my mindset is still constantly evolving and ever changing to deal with the realities of modern life outside.

    Knowing that I can get by with very little has been a huge blessing and helps me reflect on my situation with positivity, in fact when I think of all that has happened, I actually feel blessed and believe that I am extremely fortunate every day of my life.

    Many self-help gurus describe gratitude as being a powerful tool to attract positive energy and believe me, 'it is', in the lead up to my "retirement" I often found my inner mantra saying things to me like *'you are worthless, everyone hates you'* but now it only says things like *'You are a good person, you are capable and caring'* which while sounding cheesy makes my life so much easier and I believe there is a flow on effect from this.

    I also had mandatory counselling as part of my parole

and one of my therapists really helped me with anger management and mindset shift with an old but simple 'reframing technique' that I apply most days whenever I find myself in traffic and there's a driver that's too cool to indicate or feels compelled to drive 15Kms under the speed limit in the right lane, and while I'll admit that it doesn't always work it is a huge help and I even use it to make the situation seem funny.

The way it works is that if you catch yourself slipping into anger, you stop take a few breathes and reassess the situation taking into account how getting angry will help- answer, it never does, and then think of a more logical way of dealing with the situation for example, maybe the guy is just having a bad day. I take it one step further when I really feel like I'm going to get angry and I think well maybe the guy just has a micro-penis, maybe the guy behaves like this as he has a major head injury, maybe the driver is busy receiving oral gratification etcetera.

We have only recently begun understanding some of the details around the workings of the human brain and as it happens it is more plastic than previously thought, meaning that we have the ability to re-wire or change our thinking by literally creating new neural pathways or taking different mental approaches to the way we deal with problems or just our thinking in general.

If I had read this fifteen years ago, I would have probably been dubious, but I can vouch that this is a fact as I know my way of dealing with almost every situation has dramatically changed since my time in the can and especially thanks to compassionate Doctors and therapists that seemed to genuinely want better for me irrespective of my history.

Not long after my release I was trying to rethink my approach to the workforce and how I was going to make a living, I had a friend in Real Estate and she urged me to give it a shot as previously I had had excellent sales experience and was quite good at it.

Unfortunately, when I called to make enquiries around it stupidly, I asked what the ramifications of working with a record may be to which the call centre operator at the department of Fair Trade said 'Oh my god you can't be a real estate agent, what about my family?' and at the time I let myself get so angry and defeated that I didn't pursue it any further though years later I gave it more thought and approached the license with more discretion- not mentioning my past and did in fact secure my Certificate of registration which allows me to sell Real Estate in the state of issue, technically you aren't supposed to be able to attain the license as having a record precludes you working in the industry though as previously mentioned in this country the only people capable of a real background check are government departments and while the Department of Fair Trade are a government department I doubt they have the budget or time to screen every applicant and since the issuing of my certificate I have passed the ten-year threshold in any event which does not preclude you from working in the industry.

As it turns out I didn't end up having much of a crack at real estate due to the fact that when I was hired by a prestigious firm I had to work under a very lazy individual with some very major character flaws and for the money I was making it just wasn't worth it, while I know that the long term rewards may have been worth it, fighting the urge to tell a toxic person to get fucked everyday made the decision for me.

These days I still work as a PAYG, pay as you go employee, for the previously mentioned family operation, though I spend most of my waking hours reading about, thinking about and listening to Podcasts about property, thanks to the lessons learned on surviving with scarcity I was able to grow and save a small deposit eventually.

At the time of writing, I am working on my sixth investment property, the previous five are all freestanding residential houses on large blocks located throughout Australia, some regional, some capital cities.

Circling back to the plasticity of the brain I honestly believe that constantly thinking about property has allowed me to manifest the properties I own and that this new way of thinking has guided me well away from any future trouble as I no longer gravitate to negative people, or anything that may lead to law breaking behaviour.

It's funny that I spent two years of my life incarcerated and learning about how wrong I was over a half share in an amount that today I see as trivial, Robert Kiyosaki wrote that his Rich Dad said he never broke the law to get rich as it was so simple to make more money without being a criminal, and you know something, he was right.

My portfolio is gaining momentum as it is not only accruing capital growth but paying a positive cashflow too that allows me to cycle the surplus back into the debt and/or bank more cash meaning by the time I buy one property I have built enough growth to extract equity and buy another one or if I so choose, I can use equity release to pay for some fancy toy, which I would never do as I have been training myself to only buy appreciating assets not doodads as Kiyosaki calls them, being in this situation is pure heaven after the places I've found myself in the past, not having to worry about money and having a clear conscience, allows me to focus on the future and how to engineer retirement and what that is going to look like. Right now, the rent roll for my five properties, is just over one hundred and three thousand dollars a year minus outgoings and at this rate the properties will be unencumbered by the time I retire, really retire, and future properties won't be far behind and of course if they too are positively geared then some debt doesn't really matter, all that matters is that myself and my significant other will be financially free to travel and do what we feel like doing in retirement, though to be honest I don't think I will ever retire, if it isn't Real Estate or development I think I will spend a lot of time trading on the Australian Stock Exchange, which I do regularly and have done successfully for a while now, I also dabble in other markets too like the New York, London and Shanghai Stock

Exchanges.

We won't be doing any of this from a private jet or anything but we will be comfortable and with the financial forecast that our portfolios have it is only getting better, at the risk of sounding cheesy again, I do give regularly to some select charities and I find that this also has a great flow on effect in fact it makes me truly believe in karma as the more people I help the better I feel and the more luck I have. My financial situation improving will only aid me to help even more people and the success of this book will also aid in helping those in need so thank you for reading.